BEFORE THE CRISIS

John M. Montgomery

Vision
House

Ventura, CA U.S.A.

Scripture quotations are from the *New American Standard Bible*, © The Lockman Foundation 1960, 1962, 1963, 1968, 1971, 1972, 1973, 1975, 1977. Used by permission.

BEFORE THE CRISIS: Can Your Church Stand Up To An Audit?

Copyright © 1982 by Vision House Publishers,
Ventura, California 93003

Library of Congress Catalog Card Number 82-0217
ISBN 0-88449-086-6

First printing, July 1982

Printed in the United States of America.

DEDICATION

To my wife, Sandy—who prayed me
into the Kingdom. God has surely
blessed us.

ACKNOWLEDGMENTS

Credit must be given to:

Ted Engstrom and Ed Dayton—thanks for your monthly efforts in the *Christian Leadership Letter*.

Christian Ministries Management Association— a ministry whose time has come.

Christian Outreach Center, Hillsboro, Missouri— for continuing to reach out to the rural pastor. Bless you!

John M. Musgrave—your support and integrity were always there.

Nancy Cloud—for your first editing job with a first-time author. Together we have learned!

CONTENTS

FOREWORD

The Christian church faces a major crisis today: the change in the government's attitude towards charitable organizations. For years sincere pastors and church leaders through naiveté have been in violation of tax laws. Hence, the state has viewed the church with much skepticism.

Before the Crisis gives the reader a picture of the all-too-often misarranged financial affairs of a pastor and his church. It is hoped that this picture, together with the author's observations on planning, will shed some true Christian light on the unwary one's way.

John Montgomery puts in simple language the kind of information that the church leadership needs to know. He deals forthrightly with subjects involving the law which, for the most part, may be found in the Internal Revenue Code and Social Security laws. It is not the author's intent to give legal advice. The reader is directed to seek his own legal adviser for guidance in such matters.

I highly recommend that every pastor, church leader, and concerned lay person read this book and apply its principles.

Dick Erickson, LL.B., CLU
Vice-President and Counsel
First Meridian Financial Corporation
Newport Beach, California

PREFACE

Research for this book began in 1977 because a number of church leaders were unable to find answers to questions they had regarding their stewardship responsibility toward their flocks. In the complex world of corporations and taxes, with the vast number of reporting forms needed, these shepherds were at a loss to find help. Even large nonprofit/tax-exempt organizations with business managers were unable to find help. The information was written in legalese, and for a pastor not trained in these matters, it might as well have been Greek. (In most cases, the pastor would have made more sense out of the Greek.)

Not only was it difficult to determine what the church as a corporation must do to obey the law, but the pastor found that his personal responsibilities in the form of Social Security, taxes, and housing allowances were a maze of paperwork. In many cases, even his tax man did not understand the peculiarities of these subjects as they related to ministers of the gospel.

Very few pastors, evangelists, or teachers have any training or background in management of nonprofit corporations. To make the organizations function correctly, pastors have to rely on others who may know little more than they do about corporate makeup or responsibility.

Do you know that throughout the United States today no more than 10 percent of active businesses function as corporations? Yet, in order for an organization to receive tax-exempt status, it should incorporate and function as a corporation.

Assuming that a tax-exempt corporation has been formed and the pastor has a church board, are there other matters to be considered? What about the requirements under the Social Security Act? Is the clerk or secretary keeping proper records? Is anyone sure who is self-employed and who is an employee? What must be considered income and what shouldn't be? Has the pastor filed for an exemption from self-employment tax without really understanding what he has done? Does the minister file his estimated tax forms each year? Would the church be embarrassed by an IRS audit of its minister's housing allowance? What does the IRS say about pastors or staff members who write books or make cassettes that are sold or promoted by the exempt organization?

Could your organization stand up to an audit? The church's intent has never been to do anything wrong, but most church organizations do not know what is required of them. Many do not know the problems they would encounter in an audit because they have not sought competent legal advice or, at least, learned about their responsibilities under the law.

Remember, it is the responsibility of ministers and lay people alike to fulfill the laws of our land. It is my hope that this book will help you answer many of the questions posed. If you have additional questions, please seek competent legal advice before the crisis—before the IRS comes to audit

CHAPTER 1

Before What Crisis?

I am told that the word *crisis* in Chinese is defined as a "dangerous opportunity." The *Random House Dictionary* defines *crisis* as "a condition of instability, as in social, economic, or political affairs, leading to a decisive change."[1] The Greek word *krisis* loosely translates as "decision."

I believe the Christian church is facing a crisis today: the change in attitude of the government as it relates to charitable organizations, religious and otherwise.

Previously, the attitude of the government has been favorable to churches, as indicated in the first paragraph of the Treasury Department's Publication 561.

> Our Federal Government recognizes that gifts to religious, educational, charitable, scientific, and literary organizations have contributed significantly to the welfare of our nation; and our tax laws are designed to encourage such giving.[2]

However, in recent years, a real difficulty has arisen when government authorities have attempted to define the place of the church. The First Amendment forbids government entanglement with, or involvement in, the activities of the church.[3] A definition of church would be helpful, but on the other hand this is not possible because even a definition could be considered involvement. What a predicament man finds himself in. To define church is a violation, but not to establish criteria or guidelines opens the door to every type of charlatan. When is a church not a church? When is an organization qualified to call itself a church? The sacred institutions can no longer be relied upon to conform to the old traditional models. The subject is further complicated by the greed of some self-proclaimed gurus and their elaborate schemes to avoid taxes through religious exemptions.

Tax Reform

As Congress and the Treasury Department look to new tax legislation, we are bound to see tax-exempt organizations become a target for reform. I am sorry to say reform, or demand for it, can be justified by examples of excesses that can be pointed to by the reformers. Pick up an issue of *Time*, *Newsweek*, or *U.S. News & World Report*, and you will find many exposés of these excesses. For example, the November 6, 1978 issue of *U.S. News & World Report* has a five-page special report entitled "For Many, There Are Big Profits in 'Nonprofits.' " Much in the article is true and needs to be discussed. The irony of it is the Christian church is lumped right in with the phonies. The word *nonprofit* strikes a sympathetic chord in the hearts of many. It conjures up images of charities operating on limited budgets with a volunteer staff and bare offices. In many churches and exempt organizations this is true, but we must realize there are some that are not "bare-bones."

Today, there are more than 800,000 recognized tax-exempt organizations, and this number is rapidly increasing. There are over 50,000 applications for exemption filed each year. And, all too often, the reason for the rush to nonprofit status is profit! From the special report in *U.S. News & World Report* we read:

About 37 million Americans donate their services each year to charities and other voluntary organizations that spend about 29 billion dollars annually, the *bulk* of it for worthwhile causes.

But frequently these operations are something else again. Under the label "nonprofit" are organizations that are said to—

- Pay their executives fat salaries and allow them generous fringe benefits. . . .
- Serve as fronts for commercial enterprises. . . .
- Enjoy special mailing privileges and property-tax breaks that give them a competitive edge against taxpaying establishments.
- Engage in wasteful and sometimes fraudulent fundraising with little accountability to the public. . . .

Says former Internal Revenue Commissioner Sheldon Cohen: "Nonprofits are a whole can of worms that Congress has yet to look at in a broad way. I've been blowing the trumpet for years to get lawmakers to spell out clearly what should be tax-exempt and what should not."[4] (Emphasis added.)

The time has come for Christian leaders and pastors to put their legal and financial houses in order. If they do not, there will be an increase in embarrassing investigations. In most cases, these investigations will be justified. It is time for us to study and learn to avoid the crisis that looms ahead.

I want to discuss two areas where there have already been embarrassing investigations. The church has been disobedient to the law; consequently, its witness to the community has been destroyed.

Securities

The first area deals with securities law. It seems that churches are in a constant building program; the need for larger school facilities is never ending. It is impossible to build or expand without money. Church facilities are not, by their nature, a good investment for conventional lending institutions. The cash flow of a church is hard to substantiate. Thus, churches are often in the position of borrowing funds from the public or from the membership in order to continue to grow. The problem is: Most churches that raise funds by means of loans from the public or members, or by the use of a "trust account" or "revocable donation contract," are probably involved in the issuance of securities.

What is a security? "The word 'security' is defined very broadly in the federal statute: The term 'security' means any note, stock, treasury stock, bond, debenture, evidence of indebtedness. . . ."[5] Suffice it to say, a church that has given a promissory note or any other evidence of indebtedness to anyone has dealt in securities. The problem of securities becomes greater when the church or ministry starts borrowing or accepting funds into a trust from a number of people. It is at this point that the church may be dealing in a public offering, and unless the church has applied for and received permission from the proper authorities, it probably is violating a number of securities and banking laws.

I would like to tell about a true situation that developed into a horror story for a church in Northern California. In the early 1970s, the rapid growth of this church made a new facility necessary. A construction loan for $1 million was sought, but a reasonable financing package was not available. Then the church staff discovered that seven or eight churches in their denomination were using a "trust fund" to acquire property and finance expansion. It was assumed that the trust fund method was acceptable and within the limits of the law.

The church leadership decided to use the trust fund method for their building project. A brochure was prepared, spelling out the detailed workings of the trust. A document was printed resembling a stock certificate, and an account was opened at a local bank. An announcement was made to the congregation that the church would accept deposits into the trust from members and friends of the church. The interest earned on deposited money was to be more than the current interest rate available from banks or savings and loans. It was stated that a reserve, larger than that required by banks, would be maintained and that money could be withdrawn at any time.

Some five months after the trust fund began, the state corporations commissioner notified the church that he considered the trust fund to be a security and, as such, it was not exempt from registration requirements.

The letter was not shown to the congregation nor to the investors, and business continued as before. Money was deposited into the fund; interest was paid; banking records were kept; and the funds were used to finance the construction of the new facility. The cost of the new facility by that time had grown to over $5 million, and all the costs were being financed by the trust fund. The congregation and the leadership took great pride in the fact that this church building was one of the largest facilities in the state.

The Department of Corporations of the State of California issued a letter regarding trust agreements (Release No. 3-C) which applied with two exceptions. Release 3-C limited indebtedness to an amount that could be serviced by one-third of weekly receipts and required a separate fund to service principal and interest. The church still had to show financial capability to service the debt. Acquisition of land and construction costs had to be financed primarily through some means other than the trust fund. The church also had to disclose that return of funds depended on the church's financial condition, and the offering was to be limited to present members of the church.[6] Five months later the Department of Corporations sent a new and more stringent draft release. Under the terms of the new release, the trust form could not be used, and the reserve fund had to be administered by a bank or a savings and loan. There were other restrictions included in the draft release.

The church decided that it could not comply with the requirements as spelled out by the commissioner and that the Department of Corporations could not move against it without acting against many other existing church trust funds. Note that the question of right or wrong or the reasons for the requirements were not considered. The primary consideration seemed to be: "Can we do it and not get caught or get into trouble?"

Despite the obvious violations of the Department of Corporations requirements, the fund continued to function for almost four more years until the Department of Banking ordered the fund to stop accepting deposits.

The local church was not alone in its culpability; the denomination's district and headquarter offices were both aware of the trust fund and did not disapprove or offer any help or restraint. In fact, the church was encouraged by the district office, inasmuch as the trust fund method of financing had worked well for the other churches in the district.

Let me quote from *Legal Guidelines for Christian Organizations*.

California has required for sometime that nonprofit organizations register and obtain a permit before offering securities for sale to the public. The California corporations code provides that it is unlawful for any issuer to offer or sell in California any security unless the sale is either qualified or exempt. As with the federal statute, the word "security" is defined broadly in the California corporate securities law and includes, among other things, any note, bond, debenture, or evidence of indebtedness. There is an exemption for any security of an issuer organized exclusively for religious or charitable purposes and not for pecuniary profits, but this exemption specifically *excludes* the offer and sale of any evidences of indebtedness, whether interest bearing or not.

At a 1976 conference of the Christian Legal Society, a representative of the California securities division stated:

> The offering of promissory note, or other evidences of indebtedness (by nonprofit corporations), is a potential problem and requires regulation for a number of reasons. First, the church might over-extend itself and issue more notes than it is able to service as to interest and principal, in addition to any other debt that it may have. Second, it may not have made satisfactory arrangements for interest and principal as it becomes due. Third, the purchaser may not be given adequate disclosure of the financial condition of the church, the use of the proceeds, his rights as a note holder, and the nature of the note.[7]

It can readily be seen that the State of California has taken a hard line regarding the church and trust funds. All churches would be well advised to seek proper counsel prior to borrowing from the congregation or setting up a trust fund, regardless of the state in which the church is located.

One last comment must be made regarding the Northern California church and its trust fund problem. After the cease order, it was found that the fund was virtually out of money. Because of strife within the congregation, an amicable agreement for repayment could not be reached. When the problem reached its peak, the church was forced into bankruptcy, and it is now trying to settle its debt, which is over $5 million. The witness to the community has been destroyed, and the congregation has been split. The damage has been done; the credibility of a great many church leaders has been destroyed. In the end, the plans for buildings, which just a few years ago were designed to "glorify God," have become a nightmare. The church sits almost empty for everyone to see. How Satan must enjoy all that has happened.

Let me tell you about some other events, lest you think I

am singling out just one church. In Colorado a church raised funds through an issue of bonds to build a nursing home. Six years later when the nursing home had not been completed, it was discovered that the money had been spent instead for television and other media costs. The financial condition of the church had not been disclosed to investors, and eventually bankruptcy proceedings took place.

In Ohio a religious organization that included a church raised over $12 million through the use of notes which it could not repay. This organization was charged with scheming to defraud the noteholders because it did not disclose its financial condition to investors.

A minister in Oregon sold investment certificates throughout the United States. At maturity the certificates could not be redeemed because of a lack of funds, and the minister was charged with failure to comply with securities law, misrepresentation, and illegally diverting over $3 million to corporations which he owned. Over 7,000 investors faced the potential loss of their investments.

The list goes on and on, and, in almost every case, the problems stem in part from the desire of leadership to be bigger and more grand than the other guy. This success syndrome has caused Christian leadership to lose sight of the purpose of the church. Nowhere in God's Word do we find that success is measured by bigger buildings, bigger programs, or self-promotion of people. It is not considered success when a ministry goes bankrupt or damages the cause of the Great Commission by either breaking the law knowingly or by being naive.

Inurement and Self-Promotion

This brings me to the next area of disobedience of the

law that will result in poor witness as well as embarrassment: inurement and its companion, self-promotion.

Inurement is an action that becomes beneficial or advantageous to the one who is involved in the activity. Self-promotion is defined as advancement in rank, dignity, or position using one's own approval as the standard of performance.

Revenue Ruling 55-231, CB 1955-1, 72 makes it very clear that "promoting the work of an author who was one of the organization's founders is a form of inurement." An essential requisite for tax-exemption is that no part of the organization's net earnings inure to the benefit of any private individual. In recent months I have seen a flood of books and tapes being promoted in church publications, most of which have been mailed nonprofit bulk rate. If these books and/or tapes have been written or made by a staff member, and if the proceeds of the sale of these books or tapes are given to the staff member, that staff member and the exempt organization have been involved in inurement. Inurement can be a cause for revocation of tax-exempt status.

For a more blatant example of these problems, I offer you this situation which developed in California where a large church is headquartered. The state has contended that church officials were siphoning off church funds for their personal use. The state alleged that the pastor-general was spending money far too lavishly and his chief adviser was unduly benefiting from his own position; the latter had a contract for $200,000 annually, with unlimited expenses. The adviser kept homes in Beverly Hills, Pasadena, and Tucson, all of which were financed initially by the church. The state cited other alleged extravagances, including credit card excesses; there was one charge for $22,571 at a Paris hotel. Purchases of antiques, paintings, and other lavish gifts were made from church funds. The state attempted to correct alleged fraudulent diversion of assets by the church; the state attorney general had charged that since 1975 leaders of the church being investigated had diverted at least $1 million annually.

In the June 3, 1980 issue of the *Los Angeles Times* it was reported that an "evangelist . . . who last September 24 said his television ministry was $3.2 million in debt, has purchased with his two sons, a home and condominiums near Palm Beach, Fla., for $650,000 with a $177,500 cash down payment." True or not, the damage has been done. Again, from the *Los Angeles Times* May 4, 1980 issue came this news item, "Gifts of equity in home to church official questioned, financial arrangements for retiring Methodist Bishop . . . disputed among church members." This article describes a Methodist Church that wanted to give the $44,000 equity in a home to its retiring bishop and to raise an additional $85,000 to pay off the mortgage. Before the almost full-page article is finished, the bishop, who has spent over forty years in the ministry, is made to appear as the bad guy.

Again, the problem is lack of knowledge and naiveté in a situation which never should have arisen. Ignorance of the law is no defense!

CHAPTER NOTES

1. *Random House Dictionary of the English Language—The Unabridged Edition*, s.v. "crisis."

2. U.S., Department of the Treasury, *Valuation of Donated Property*, IRS Publication 561, 1977, p. 1.

3. U.S. Constitution, First Amendment, "Congress shall make no law respecting an establishment of religion, or prohibiting the free exercise thereof; or abridging the freedom of speech, or of the press; or the right of the people peaceably to assemble, and to petition Government for a redress of grievances."

4. Lawrence Maloney, "For Many, There Are Big Profits in 'Nonprofits,'" *U.S. News & World Report* 85 (November 6, 1978), p. 45.

5. William H. Ellis and Joel H. Paget, *Legal Guidelines for Christian Organizations* (Oak Park, Ill.: Christian Legal Society, 1977), p. 21.

6. State of California, Department of Corporations, Release No. 3-C, October 3, 1974.

7. *Legal Guidelines*, pp. 22-23.

CHAPTER 2

The Corporation as a Legal Entity

You and I eventually will go to be with the Lord. Our tents will cease to exist. The life of a corporation, however, is continuous and ceases to exist only when those in control, the board of directors, have taken steps to cause it to end. An important point is that the control rests with the board of directors. To make this point clear, let us look at the basics of corporate structure and the difference between profit and nonprofit organizations. This will be a basic outline without great detail.

Stockholders/Board of Directors

For an example of a profit-making corporation, let us take two men who are plumbers and who decide to join forces to become one business. Their lawyer advises against partnership for a number of reasons, but he does advise them to incorporate. Let us also assume that plumber Al has more equipment, a newer truck, and more accounts receivable than plumber Bob. Each is contributing his assets to the corporation. The attorney drafts the articles and bylaws and files them with the state. Then he meets with Al and Bob to issue stock in their new corporation. Since Al put more and better equipment into the corporation, the attorney issues 60 percent of the stock to Al and 40 percent to Bob. Now, since this is a profit-making corporation, the majority stockholder(s) controls the board and thus controls the corporation. Bob has his minority stock position, but Al is the boss. This is an ultra-simplified example for the sake of illustration, and in real life it would not necessarily develop this way.

The Need for Incorporation

Now, in the case of a profit-making corporation, we have seen that the board is in control. What about the stockholders of the nonprofit corporation? The answer is, there are no stockholders. In fact, to be exempt, the articles must clearly state that no part of the net earnings of the corporation shall inure to the benefit of, or be distributable to, its members, trustees, officials, or other private persons. Thus, we can see that the board is still in charge, but the corporation is not organized to generate profits for stockholders. Rather, the corporation is organized for a tax-exempt purpose and its bylaws must specifically state that no individual is to profit from the existence of the corporation.

We remarked in the preface that fewer than 10 percent of active business endeavors function as corporations. Yet, in order to qualify for tax exemption, the church and para-church organizations must be a legal entity (a corporation). Each application for recognition of exemption must be accompanied by a conformed copy of its organization's certificate of incorporation, constitution, articles of association, trust indenture, or other enabling instruments. It is possible to function as something other than an incorporated entity (i.e., trust or association). However, the corporate path seems to be the one of least resistance and most often will fit the needs of the church and para-church organizations.

To illustrate, let us create a hypothetical situation involving a character we will call Rev. E. Van Gelizer. Let us make him a well-known spiritual leader and evangelist. In his earlier years, after completing his schooling, he set about the task to which he was called. As he went about his ministry, the problem of taxation did not even enter his mind. His message was heard by more and more people, and his ministry grew. People began to send him money and gifts. His ministry continued to grow until he found himself preaching before convention center crowds. Gifts continued to come in cash and checks. And, as fast as the money came in, Rev. Van Gelizer sent it back out to further the Great Commission.

Enter the IRS. Some friends have made large contributions by check to Rev. Van Gelizer, and they deducted the amounts on their income tax returns. The IRS investigated and found that, while Rev. Van Gelizer was honest, he was not a tax-exempt organization for which income tax deductions are allowed. The contributors' deductions were disallowed, causing a bad witness. Rev. Van Gelizer was aghast. Intent upon rectifying the situation, he sought the advice of an attorney, who recommended that a nonprofit corporation be formed. They did this in the name of Van Gelizer Evangelical Ministries, Inc., and filed for a tax-exempt status. Once the Internal Revenue Service granted the exemption, Rev. Van Gelizer's organization functioned under the umbrella of a corporate structure free from tax and contributions to the organization were now deductible.

IRS Guidelines for Church Exemption

In most states, a church does not need to incorporate nor file for tax-exempt status. It is exempt simply because it is a church. This can lead to some very touchy situations, however. For example, what constitutes a church? Are you sure your fellowship group qualifies? Because of the farce being perpetrated by such organizations as the Universal Life Church, the Temple of Bacchus, and others, the IRS is taking a tough stand against what it considers abuses of tax relief designated for churches. At times, the IRS has ruled against the use of a home, store, or garage as a church building.

The Rev. Van Gelizer might have taken the position that his group was a church, and he might have been right, but could he meet these guidelines as published in IRS News Release IR-1930?

GUIDELINES FOR IRS AGENTS. Since beliefs and practices are so varied, IRS cannot define a church, but resorts to a case-by-case approach to determine whether an organization is a church, says IRS Commissioner Jerome Kurtz. IRS looks at 14 elements:

(1) a distinct legal existence;
(2) a recognized creed and form of worship;
(3) a definite and distinct ecclesiastical government;
(4) a formal code of doctrine and discipline;
(5) a distinct religious history;
(6) a membership not associated with any other church or denomination;
(7) a complete organization of ordained ministers ministering to their congregations;
(8) ordained ministers selected after completing prescribed courses of study;
(9) a literature of its own;
(10) established places of worship;
(11) regular congregations;
(12) regular religious services;
(13) Sunday schools for the religious instruction of the young; and
(14) schools for the preparation of its ministers.[1]

How many of these fourteen qualifications does your un-incorporated fellowship (church) meet? Could your group stand up to an IRS audit? Organizations do not need to meet all these standards, but the more they do, the better chance they have of being exempt as a church. A recent publication on taxation arrived on my desk. The heading in bold print caught my eye: "Form-Your-Own Churches Are High on the IRS Hit List and It Intends to Go After Their Founders."[2]

One last comment regarding Rev. Van Gelizer and his situation: You will remember that the corporation formed was Van Gelizer Evangelical Ministries, Inc. Now let us assume that Rev. Van Gelizer and his board did not elect to become a church, but wanted to stay in the evangelistic field without a church affiliation. Under these circumstances, the corporation would have had to file for nonprofit status and then request exemption. Remember, it is only a church that is not required to file for exemption, and this is only true in some states.

Corporation—Liability or Protection?

Since it is so important to maintain a good witness, and since some delight in finding fault with any organization or person professing to be Christian, it becomes important to protect both the image of the individual and the Christian name. If you recall, we discussed the fact that a corporation is an entity of its own; it is not Rev. Van Gelizer. He may be the president of the corporation, he may be the key person in its function, but he is not the corporation.

For example, if Rev. Van Gelizer were to leave his ministry, the corporation would continue to exist unless the board of directors took steps to dissolve it. The fact that the corporation is separate from Rev. Van Gelizer has another advantage. The corporation is responsible to itself. So, if through negligence, the pastor or a member of his staff should fail to accurately report his own income tax, or if he should on his own violate the law in any way, it would not affect Van Gelizer Evangelical Ministries, Inc. (except by association). Additionally, if anyone within the corporation acted wrongly or illegally, Rev. Van Gelizer would not be hurt directly. It can readily be seen that this is very different from what would happen if all activities of Rev. Van Gelizer were carried out in his name without the protection of the corporate umbrella. Any unlawful act, intended or not, could lead to a forced shutdown of the Reverend's work; his mission would cease, or would at the very least be adversely affected.

The corporation also has continuity of life beyond that of the founder. If Rev. Van Gelizer, after a long and happy career of evangelistic work, should retire or go to be with the Lord, the corporation would not go with him (no, he can't take it with him). The corporation would carry on the mission. Nothing would change, not even the name. All that would be necessary is the appointment of a new minister to take his place, and there would be continuity.

It should be noted that, while Rev. Van Gelizer was president of the corporation, he was not necessarily running the organization. He was involved in the decision making and was the spiritual leader; however, the board of directors was charged with the responsibility of running the corporation. When the new minister arrived, he did not take over; the board continued to function just as it had before. Contrast that with a non-corporate organization led by one person, and the advantage of corporate management can readily be seen. Rev. Van Gelizer was called to be an evangelist, not a businessman. Having the centralization of management in the board of directors frees him to continue to be an evangelist, while the board functions as the business head.

There is good reason for the IRS to take a dim view of a

person, Christian or otherwise, who receives contributions for a particular cause, but who keeps no records of the income or expenses. As honest as the person in charge may be, the IRS and the donors have a right to know how much was received and where the money went. The contributions were not given to increase the standard of living of the leader nor for his personal investment, but for the cause that was espoused. If the money should become the personal gain of an individual, it is certainly not nonprofit; and the IRS has the right to tax those dollars as income. Contributors are entitled to take charitable deductions on their income tax returns for genuine gifts of cash or property to qualified organizations.

Qualified Organizations

Now, how do we define qualified 501(c)(3) organizations? Let us look at what constitutes a qualified 501(c)(3) organization. (See the Organization Reference Chart on page 32.[3])

Basically the organizations fall into two groups. The first group includes "50 percent"-type organizations, which are churches, schools, hospitals, and governmental agencies. It also may include organizations that normally receive a substantial part of their support from governmental agencies, the general public, and certain private foundations, commonly referred to as operating foundations, "community" or "pooled fund" foundations. A 50 percent-type organization allows the non-corporate contributor to deduct up to 50 percent of his adjusted gross income in the year of his gift, with five years of carryover of the excess.

The second group comprises all other types of organizations, including private foundations, to which contributions are deductible. These organizations are referred to as

ORGANIZATION REFERENCE CHART

Section of 1954 code	Description of organization	General nature of activities	Form No.	Annual return to be filed	Contribution allowable
501(c)(1)	Corporations Organized Under Act of Congress (including Federal Cred it Unions	Instrumentalities of the U S	No Form	None	Yes. if made for exclusively public purpos- es
501(c)(2)	Title Holding Corporation For Ex- empt Organization	Holding title to property of an ex- empt organization	1024	990¹	No²
501(c)(3)	Religious. Educational. Charitable. Scientific. Literary. Testing for Public Safety. Foster Certain National or In- ternational Amateur Sports Competi- tion. or Prevention of Cruelty to Children or Animals Organizations	Activities of nature implied by des- cription of class of organization	1024	990 or 990-PF¹	Generally. Yes
501(c)(4)	Civic Leagues. Social Welfare Org- ganizations. and Local Associations of Employees	Promotion of community welfare. Charitable. educational or recrea- tional	1024	990¹	Generally No² ³
501(c)(5)	Labor. Agricultural. and Horticultural Organizations	Educational or instructive. the pur- pose being to improve conditions of work. and to improve products and efficiency	1024	990¹	No²
501(c)(6)	Business Leagues. Chambers of Commerce. Real Estate Boards. Etc.	Improvement of business conditions of one or more lines of business	1024	990¹	No²
501(c)(7)	Social and Recreation Clubs	Pleasure. recreation. social activities	1024	990¹	No¹
501(c)(8)	Fraternal Beneficiary Societies and Associations	Lodge providing for payment of life. sickness. accident. or other benefits to members	1024	990¹	Yes. if used for Sec 501(c)(3) purposes
501(c)(9)	Voluntary Employees Beneficiary Associations (Including Federal Em- ployees Voluntary Beneficiary Asso- ciations formerly covered by section 501(c)(10)	Providing for payment of life. sick- ness. accident. or other benefits to members	1024	990¹	No²
501(c)(10)	Domestic Fraternal Societies and Associations	Lodge devoting its net earnings to charitable. fraternal. and other speci- fied purposes No life. sickness. or accident benefits to members	1024	990¹	Yes. if used for Sec 501(c)(3) purposes
501(c)(11)	Teachers Retirement Fund Associa- tions	Teachers association for payment of retirement benefits	No Form	990¹	No²
501(c)(12)	Benevolent Life Insurance Associa- tions. Mutual Ditch or Irrigation Com- panies. Mutual or Cooperative Tele- phone Companies. Etc	Activities of a mutually beneficial nature similar to those implied by the description of class of organization	1024	990¹	No²
501(c)(13)	Cemetery Companies	Burials and incidental activities	1024	990¹	Generally. Yes
501(c)(14)	State Chartered Credit Unions. Mu tual Reserve Funds	Loans to members Exemption as to building and loan associations and cooperative banks repealed by Rev- enue Act of 1951. affecting all years after 1951	No	990¹	No²
501(c)15)	Mutual Insurance Companies or As- sociations	Providing insurance to members sub- stantially at cost	1024	990¹	No²
501(c)(16)	Cooperative Organizations to Finan- ce Crop Operations	Financing crop operations in con- junction with activities of a marketing purchasing association	No Form	990¹	No¹
501(c)(17)	Supplemental Unemployment Ben- efit Trusts	Provides for payment of supplement- al unemployment compensation be- nefits	1024	990	No²
501(c)(18)	Employee Funded Pension Trust (created before June 25. 1959)	Payment of benefits under a pen- sion plan funded by employees	No Form	990¹	No·
501(c)(19)	Post or Organization of War Veterans	Activities implied by nature of organ- ization	1024	990¹	Yes
501(c)(20)	Group Legal Services Plan Organi- izations	Providing prepaid personal (non- business) legal services for employ- ees	1024	990¹	No⁴
501(d)	Religious and Apostolic Associations	Regular business activities Com- munal religious community	No Form	1065	No²
501(e)	Cooperative Hospital Service Or- ganizations	Performs cooperative services for hospitals	1023	990¹	Yes
501(f)	Cooperative Service Organizations of Operating Educational Organiza- tions	Performs collective investment ser- vices for educational organizations	1023	990	Yes

¹For exceptions to the fi requirement see the instruct for Forms 990 and 990—A

²An organization exempt in a Subsection of Code Sec other than (c)(3) may establ a charitable fund. contributi to which are deductible Su fund must itself meet the req ments of section 501(c)(3) the related notice requireme of section 508(a)

³Contributions to volunteer companies and similar organ tions are deductible. but on made for exclusively pul purposes

⁴See Chapter 14

"20 percent" corporations. For the sake of our discussion, we will concern ourselves with only the 50 percent type.

A common characteristic of all exempt corporations is that no part of their income may inure to the benefit of any individual. This refers to ownership, not to salaries or other forms of compensation. However, excessive salaries or other forms of excessive compensation (e.g., travel, clothing, unlimited use of credit cards) may void a corporation's exempt status on the grounds that a part of the corporation's earnings inures to the benefit of an individual.

Nonprofit and/or Tax-Exempt

Confusion exists when we use the terms *nonprofit corporation* and *tax-exempt corporation*. An organization may be nonprofit under applicable state law, but this does not mean that it is tax-exempt. Nonprofit status may be, in effect, a prerequisite for exemption, but by itself does not confer exemption. Neither does exemption from state or local taxes establish that an organization is organized and operated exclusively for one or more federal exempt purposes. In other words, until an organization qualifies for and receives exempt status from the Treasury Department, it is not exempt from federal taxes.

I want to remind you that churches do not need to make application for federal exemption in many states. However, it may be a good thing to do anyway. In order to be listed in the IRS publication of exempt organizations, your ministry must have filed for and received exemption. If your organization is not a church, or if you are not sure what your ministry is qualified to be, and it is claiming an exemption, it would be wise to read very carefully *How to Apply for Recognition of Exemption for an Organization* (IRS Publication 557). The first paragraph of the first chapter includes these instructions:

> An organization that claims to be exempt, but has not yet estab-
> lished its exempt status, should file Form 990, *Return of Organi-
> zation Exempt From Income Tax*. In such cases, the organization
> must indicate on Form 990 that the return is being filed in the
> belief the organization is exempt under section 501(a) of the
> Code, but that the Internal Revenue Service has not yet recog-
> nized such exemption.[4]

No organization may claim exemption from tax unless it
is first determined to be an exempt organization. It must
submit proof of exemption to the IRS district director for
the district in which the corporation's principal place of
business is located. To file for tax-exempt status under Section 501(c)(3) of the Internal Revenue Code, it must use
IRS Form 1023 (see Appendix). Once the exempt character
of a corporation has been established and the IRS has issued a determination letter, the organization must file an
annual information return using Form 990 (see Appendix).
Churches, however, are exempt from the information return reporting rules.

Unrelated Business Income

An exempt organization is not subject to tax on any of its
income except unrelated business income, which is income generated by activities not related to the purpose for
which the corporation was founded. That income must be
reported on IRS Form 990-T (see Appendix). For example,
if your church received a toy manufacturing company as a
gift, the profits of the company would be unrelated business income and would be taxable.

The area of unrelated business income has been responsible for a great deal of confusion in the last few years. Few
understand what is and what is not unrelated business income. The first consideration must be unfair competition.

The tax-free status of Section 501 organizations enables them to use their profits tax free to expand operations, while their competitors can expand only with the profits remaining after taxes are paid. Some tax-free organizations, in effect, have used their tax-exemptions to buy an ordinary business. They have acquired the business with little or no investment on their own part and paid for it in installments out of subsequent earnings. This is unfair competition. An exemption will not be revoked or denied in this case if the tax that is imposed on unrelated business income is paid. If an exempt organization has unrelated business income, and if that organization files a tax Form 990T and pays its taxes on such income, it is conforming to the Internal Revenue Code. Prior to the Tax Reform Act of 1969, churches were not subject to the unrelated business income provisions. However, churches were involved in various types of commercial activities, and the Tax Reform Act made the income from unrelated business activities subject to tax.

It should be noted that some exclusions from unrelated business income are allowed. An in-depth study of these exclusions cannot be a part of this chapter. If you suspect your organization might be involved in unrelated business, you should discuss it with competent advisers, referring them to Internal Revenue Code 513(a).

Group Exemptions

In many incorporated religious organizations, it is not uncommon for one to find a separately incorporated subsidiary. While the parent corporation may be exempt, it does not follow that the subsidiary corporation is automatically exempt. The inclusion of the subsidiary's financial information on the parent organization's information return does not satisfy the reporting requirement. In certain situations, the parent organization's reporting exemption does not carry over to the subsidiary organization. However, a group return may be filed by a central, parent, or like organization for two or more local organizations (none of which may be private foundations) provided the local organizations are:

1. Affiliated with the central organization at the close of the central organization's annual accounting period;
2. Subject to the general supervision or control of the central organization; and
3. Exempt from a tax under a group exemption letter which is currently in effect.[5]

All three of these requirements must be met. Each local organization must annually authorize the central organization in writing to include it in the group return. It also must file annually with the central organization a declaration of the truth and completeness of the authorization and statements required under penalty of perjury. The group return is filed in addition to the separate return of the central organization. If an organization fails to file its Form 990 on or before the due date, it will have to pay $10 for each day the return is late (not to exceed $5,000). All penalties are a waste of the funds God has provided for the ministry He has given you. Be aware!

CHAPTER NOTES

1. U.S., Department of the Treasury, Internal Revenue News Release, IR-1930.

2. Patrick A. Heller, "Form-Your-Own Churches Are High on the IRS Hit List and It Intends to Go After Their Founders," *T.C. Memo*, 1978-149:4.

3. U.S., Department of the Treasury, *How to Apply for Recognition of Exemption for an Organization*, IRS Publication 557, 1978, p. 25.

4. Ibid., p. 1.

5. Ibid., p. 4.

CHAPTER 3

The IRS Audit

The IRS will want to know if your organization is engaged in the activities for which it received tax-exempt status. This intent is expressed in IRS Publication 857.

> The Internal Revenue Service recognizes the exempt status of organizations on the basis of their purposes and activities. It is the Service's duty to insure that exempt organizations continue to operate within the applicable provisions of law. For this reason, we examine returns of these organizations.[1]

Okay! Your organization receives a notice that the IRS wants to visit you. Now what? The first thought most of us would have is—why? May I assure you that you need not feel you are being singled out for persecution. The IRS examines more than 20,000 exempt organizations annually. This number is increasing as fast as the IRS can train people. Remember that there are in excess of 800,000 recognized exempt organizations in existence, and over 50,000 applications for exemptions are accepted or rejected by the IRS each year.[2] Start adding the numbers, and you will have a feel for the size of job the IRS has.

The exempt organization auditor is, for the most part, a considerate, well-trained person who is not out to "get" honest organizations. However, he is making sure that those who have claimed an exemption are truly staying within the framework of the exempt purpose.

Programmatic, Not Financial

The IRS auditor who examines your personal income tax return is looking at it from a financial point of view. The one who audits your exempt organization will be doing a programmatic audit. Programmatic means that the exempt functions or activities of your organization will be reviewed. His chief concern will be to see that your organization is staying within the boundaries of its tax-exempt purpose; however, he also will be interested in the financial aspects. The place of audit will almost always be your office, not the auditor's. He will want to make a visual inspection of your facilities for obvious reasons.

Defining the Word *Religion*

In the November 1979 issue of *Reader's Digest*, there is an article entitled "How Cults Bilk All Of Us." The subtitle capsulizes the thrust of the article: "Because they don't have to file annual financial reports with the IRS, unscrupulous sects can—and do—ignore the law with impunity. Let's close this tax loophole." The article, which is just one of many found in such publications, hits its mark.

> . . . they are able to violate the tax law by funneling tax-exempt money into profit-making businesses, and into the pockets of their leaders, many of whom live like potentates at public expense.[3]

The writer makes a good point. We are all familiar with phony religions, rip-off charities, and welfare fraud. The problem is that the term *religion* cannot be defined with precision. It has been interpreted broadly by the courts. The Supreme Court has suggested that serious Constitutional difficulties would be presented if the exempt section of the Internal Revenue Code were interpreted to exclude those beliefs that do not encompass a Supreme Being in the conventional sense, such as Taoism, Buddhism, and Secular Humanism. This being the case, it is obvious that organizations such as the Church of Scientology, ISKCON (better known as Hare Krishnas), and the Unification Church (Moonies) know how far they are able to bend the exempt organization code.

A hue and cry is developing throughout the country to "stop the crooks." The problem is: How? Should the courts decide what a church is? Do we let the courts determine what constitutes religion and what is religious? What if they decide that Christianity is not a religion or that only churches over fifty years of age should qualify for exemption?

The most sought after reform would require that all churches file annual financial reports with the IRS. Ironically the cults and crooks would probably retain advisers to find a way to go on cheating, while the traditional church, in honest naiveté, could find itself in trouble and possibly lose its exempt status. Another suggestion that has been made is do away with the tax-free status of all churches. This appears to be the direction the trend is taking us.

I point out these concerns to you here to acquaint you with the problem that the auditor faces. Remember, the auditor is not just examining churches as we know them. He is auditing every type of 501(c)(3) organization. When you are asked to produce certain items, you must understand that the auditor does not know you and he is not aware yet that you are an honest organization.

Audit Items

The first items that the agent will want to see are your articles of incorporation, bylaws, and exemption letter. If these items are in order, the agent will review various activity items such as changes in articles and bylaws, minutes, any newsletters or brochures your organization produces, your correspondence files, and other narrative reports.

The agent will have certain considerations in mind. These considerations generally fall in five areas:

1. Inurement,
2. Private benefits,
3. Illegal activities,
4. Legislative and political activities, and
5. Unrelated business income.

While the auditor of a tax-exempt organization is primarily performing a programmatic audit, he also will ask to see some, if not all, of your financial records (for example: your year-end report to members; your employment tax forms; and in some cases, specific income and expense items).[4] If your organization uses an outside accountant rather than an in-house bookkeeper, the IRS seems to be more favorably impressed. There are other specific items that the agent will request.

1. If your organization is a school, he will look for complete information as to your racial non-discrimination policy.
2. If your organization is an exempt church, he will want evidence to support your claim that a church does in fact exist.
3. He also will want to look at your control of funds and contributions to other exempt organizations.

Since the audit is generally programmatic rather than financial, what is the IRS trying to accomplish? In my opinion, the issue of revocation will be the key goal—if not now, certainly in the near future.

CHAPTER NOTES

1. U.S., Department of the Treasury, *Why Your Return Is Being Audited: Exempt Organizations*, IRS Publication 857, December 1974.

2. Lawrence Maloney, "For Many, There Are Big Profits in 'Nonprofits,'" *U.S. News & World Report* 85 (November 6, 1978), pp. 45, 52.

3. C. Williams, "How Cults Bilk All Of Us," *Reader's Digest* 115, no. 691 (November 1979), pp. 237-238.

4. Mention must be made regarding the restrictions against IRS agents conducting examinations of churches. Section 7605(c) of the Internal Revenue Code states that IRS agents must go through a preexamination process before making an audit of *churches*. The purposes of the restrictions, as spelled out in the code, are to protect churches or associations of churches from undue interference in their internal affairs through unnecessary examinations. Protection afforded the church through this section of the code is primarily that of protection related to the financial aspects of the organization. Church business managers, clerks, and pastors would be well advised to obtain a copy of this code section, read it, and be aware of this safeguard to the church.

CHAPTER 4

Designated Gifts

The subject of gifts has caused much confusion. Are designated gifts deductible? Are gifts given directly to the pastor taxable to him? These are just two of the questions addressed in this chapter.

Are They Deductible?

First, let us approach the most difficult problem of designated gifts: Are they deductible? Section 170(c) of the Internal Revenue Code defines a deductible contribution or gift as one made to or for the use of certain types of organizations and entities.[1] Notice the phrase "to or for the use of." By this definition, gifts to a needy individual, even though actuated by charitable or religious motives, are not deductible.

Often a person entering the ministry, particularly one who is leaving for the mission field, will discuss with congregations and individuals the possibility of receiving support for his ministry. When the check is made out directly to the person, it is not "to or for the use of" the exempt organization and is not a tax-deductible contribution.

What about a check made payable to an exempt organization but designated for a particular individual? The donor still may have a problem in this situation because the IRS contends that in order for a contribution to be deductible, the donation or gift must be made to an exempt organization which must "maintain control and responsibility" for the funds.[2] If the donor has the right to determine where and to whom the funds go, then it is obvious that the exempt organization does not "maintain control and responsibility" for the funds, and the contribution is not considered to be deductible.

Since church schools are becoming increasingly popular, a new area of concern regarding deductibility of gifts is arising. When a donor has children in the church school, his contribution to the church may be suspect in the eyes of the IRS, particularly if the church school does not charge tuition. Why? A gift, to be deductible, must be given without the incentive of anticipated benefits.[3] Thus a gift made to a church, where the donor has children in a free day school, may be deductible only to the extent that it exceeds the fair market value of the schooling. Even if the church does not put a price tag on the education, the IRS might.

In order for designated gifts to be deductible, the contributor must be made aware that the contribution is made to the exempt organization and not to the designee. The exempt organization must control the funds. The exempt organization cannot honor contributions as deductible where the donor appears to have a personal interest in the contribution.

Let us look at the position the IRS auditor will take in relation to designated giving. During an audit he will ask if the organization has a written policy regarding designated contributions. The policy should state that the ultimate control of the designated funds rests with the exempt organization. The auditor also will inquire as to whether the stated policy has been communicated to the donors. He more than likely will inquire about specific designated gifts, and he will make a thorough analysis of the manner in which these specific gifts were handled. If the donor is being audited, the exempt organization will be asked to furnish pertinent information and documentation regarding the gift in question.

Gifts to Pastors

Because the pastor loves his flock and the flock loves the pastor, they often show their love by giving gifts to him. The gifts can take many forms: from gifts of little financial value to large items, such as cars, pianos, and vacations. In many cases the person who helps the pastor with his tax return might forget to ask about gifts. The gifts may be from the congregation for his birthday or Christmas, or it may be a love gift from an individual member of the congregation. In most cases, these gifts are considered to be income, and this income is taxable.

Let me quote from *Commerce Clearing House* (Code Section 61):

> All compensation for personal services, regardless of the form of payment, is gross income when received, . . . marriage fees and contributions received by clergymen (unless turned over to the church) are all taxable forms of payment for personal services. A pastor's work, by its very nature qualifies him in the eyes of the code, under "compensation for personal services." A bequest which is actually payment for a taxpayer's services prior to the decedent's death, is includable in gross income (Revenue Ruling 67-375, 1967-2, CB 60).[4]

For most taxpayers, a gift is a gift and is not taxed (unless the gift is larger than $3,000). However, the clergyman is considered to be rendering personal services any time he is dealing with his congregation, individually or as a group. It is an area of taxation that has many gray areas within it. Next tax season I hope you will discuss this subject with your tax preparer. You bring up the subject, even if he does not. Remember, at audit time it is you who answers to the IRS.

Love Gifts and Merchandising

I would be remiss if I did not touch on one more problem area before leaving this discussion of gifts. We all have received letters or publications that include a statement similar to the following: For your gift of $25 or more, we will send you a love gift in return—a red letter, giant print Bible valued at $29.95. Or the offer may be a Living New Testament on tape. In some cases, the gift you receive will be dependent upon the size of the gift you send. For example, for your gift of $5, they will send you a book valued at $2.95; for your gift of $100, you will receive a tape recorder valued at $69.95; and for your gift of $1,000, they will make you a gift of a video recorder valued at $895. Does this sound like merchandising to you?

We must see what the IRS has to say about gifts in return for contributions. The IRS takes the position that the amount of deduction that is allowed is the amount in excess of the fair market value of the item received.[5] This being the case, it would seem that if I sent $25 to an exempt organization, and they sent me a Bible "worth $29.95," I would not be eligible for a deduction. If I am honest, didn't I really just buy the Bible?

If I bought the book, Bible, or tapes at the store, would I be able to claim a deduction? How do you think the owner of the local TV store would react if he knew that you could buy a video recorder from a "religious organization" and receive a tax deduction? He must compete and pay taxes. This sort of thing is not a good witness, and it is in violation of the Internal Revenue Code.

There is a way to handle this type of situation. Let me

give you an illustration of how the Center for Law and Religious Freedom handles its contributions. On the back of its information brochure, you will find an application for membership which reads in part:

> ... please enroll me as a member of the Center Lay division. Enclosed are my annual dues of $15 ($5 of the dues covers a subscription to *The Advocate* and the remainder and all other gifts are fully tax deductible).

I highly recommend this type of statement.

Churches and other exempt organizations, which hold banquets for fund raising or sell Christmas trees or other items, need to discuss the subject with a qualified tax adviser.

We need to improve our witness to the world. When you hear or see this sort of thing, inform the offending organization of the law, give them the facts in love, and let them know it concerns you.

CHAPTER NOTES

1. Internal Revenue Code Section 170(c).

2. See Revenue Ruling 75-65, IRB 1975-1, 9.

3. U.S., Department of the Treasury, *Valuation of Donated Property,* IRS Publication 561, 1977, p. 3.

4. *Commerce Clearing House,* Code Section 61.

5. Internal Revenue Code Section 170.

CHAPTER 5

Deferred Compensation

Most of us save some of our money, but do we save to save, or do we save to spend? During my last fifteen years as a financial counselor, I have made an interesting observation: Most people have been taught some form of thrift by their elders. Most consider it important to save.

Save to Save or Save to Spend?

There are all kinds of savings concepts: Christmas clubs; mutual fund clubs; saving 10 percent of all you earn; setting aside a certain percentage of your dollars first before paying the bills; and starting a savings account for Junior, etc. I am sure we have all tried to save, using one or more of the above systems. In most cases, we save a little; then something happens to our good intentions, and less and less goes into savings until one day we are not saving anything. At that point, we generally decide to start a new plan. We rationalize, "We might as well use the money we have managed to save. Besides, we need a new TV set." So, we withdraw what we have saved and we reaffirm our good intentions by starting a new plan.

The problem is: Many people save to spend, but few save to save. Most of us save, but few accumulate for the future.

Let me introduce Pastor I. Savem for this illustration. He receives a fixed salary from a church. He has a wife, two children, and a salary sufficient to provide a comfortable living. Each year Pastor and his wife make definite

plans to save some of their income, realizing that there
will come a day when they may want to retire. They have
watched others try to retire on just Social Security, and
they have seen that it is just not enough to provide a comfortable living. They are aware that college costs are rising
higher and higher. They want at least to help the children
when it is time for college. All of this takes savings, and the
Savems have not really put anything aside so far.

The Savems determine that this will be the year they
start saving for retirement. So they visit their bank to open
a savings account. The pastor compares the different types
of accounts and finds that, if he is saving to spend, a passbook account is the easiest way to go. He may put money
in and take it out at will, with no strings attached. The
passbook account pays less interest than a Certificate of
Deposit; however, a CD does not allow him to take money
out except at the end of a specified time, unless he wishes
to pay a penalty. The CD sounds a bit more like saving to
save, and so he opens a five-year Certificate of Deposit account. Pastor deposits $1,000 into this account and prom-
ises himself that he will continue to save at least $100 every
two weeks from now on. Savem feels good on the way
home. At last he has really started his savings plan.

Typical Budget

Now let us look at Savem's budget and see how hard it
was to save that thousand dollars. Rather than list each
item in his budget, we will only list the major headings.

1. RESIDENCE
   a. Rent or mortgage payment $350
      (including tax and insurance)
   b. Maintenance   20
   c. Utilities   50

d. Furniture replacement $ 10
e. Miscellaneous (e.g., personal phone)   20
2. FOOD
   a. Groceries   250
   b. Outside meals (not reimbursed)   20
3. CLOTHING
   a. Dry cleaning   10
   b. Replacement and repair   25
4. MEDICAL
   a. Doctor   10
   b. Dentist   10
   c. Medical and disability insurance   65
   d. Medications   10
5. TRANSPORTATION
   a. Car payments (or purchase fund)   90
      (church furnishes one car)
   b. Car insurance   15
   c. License   7
   d. Maintenance and repairs   10
   e. Gasoline and oil   50
   f. Other (bus, taxi)   5
6. RECREATION AND PERSONAL GROWTH
   a. Local recreation (movies, etc.)   30
   b. Family vacation   50
   c. Books, newspaper, and magazines   10
   d. Club dues and hobbies   10
   e. Education expense or savings   25
   f. Children's pocket money   8
   g. Gifts: holiday, birthday, etc.   10
7. CONTRIBUTIONS
   a. Church   100
   b. Missions   25
8. TAXES
   a. Income (federal and state)   150

9. SAVINGS
   a. Personal savings $200
   b. Mutual funds
   c. Life insurance 30
   d. Other investments
10. MISCELLANEOUS
   a. Credit card payment 10
   b. Installment payments 15
   c. Large account payments 40
   d. Personal loan payments
   e. Other, including pledges 95
   $1835

As we can see, the pastor does not live extravagantly, nor has he taken any emergency into account. Pastor Savem receives the following income:

$1,500 a month salary

$ 325 a month parsonage allowance
   auto fuel and maintenance reimbursement
   telephone reimbursement (except personal calls)

With expenses of $1,835, he appears to have almost enough to meet his obligations. It isn't difficult to find holes or low areas in his budget. But at least Pastor Savem has budgeted the $200 he promised would go to savings. How long do you think he will continue to save? It is very possible that the first emergency situation that arises will end the savings plan of Pastor Savem.

Now let me reintroduce Rev. E. Van Gelizer and present a new set of circumstances. We will use exactly the same conditions with regard to the number of children, budgeted amounts, and savings. The board of directors of his church realizes that it is difficult for anyone to save money in today's economy with its rising costs. The board members have a strong desire to have Rev. Van Gelizer continue as their pastor, and so they pass a resolution that gives Rev. Van Gelizer an employment agreement. The agreement spells out such things as car allowance, parsonage allowance, medical expense reimbursements for his family, and a deferred compensation agreement that sets aside funds for his later years. Their concern also includes the possibility that Rev. Van Gelizer could become disabled and not be able to perform his duties (insurance industry publications indicate one in five persons will become disabled). The board also knows that in the event of his premature death, his family will face difficult times; therefore, the agreement includes a death benefit.

Deferred Compensation

Let us examine the deferred compensation agreement. Rev. Van Gelizer, like Pastor Savem, would like to save at least $200 a month. In the past, he has attempted to start a savings plan many times, and he has yet to accumulate very much. His problem is typical; something always comes along that causes him to abort his plan. Realizing how hard saving is for him, the board members decide to look at what secular businesses do for their key employees.

Businesses have discovered that certain employees do not really need more salary income now because it would just mean higher personal income taxes. What employees need is a plan that will allow them to accumulate money that will not be taxed until sometime later, when their income and taxes are not so high. They also would like this accumulating money to grow. Well, if it is good for businesses, why not for pastors?

The board, with the help of counsel, draws up a deferred compensation agreement in conjunction with the employment agreement. The deferred compensation agreement states that the church (a tax-exempt, nonprofit organization) will provide for Rev. Van Gelizer an amount to be deposited monthly and held by a bank or other investment medium. The funds will remain an asset of the church and are deposited on the condition that he will stay in their employ for a specified length of time.

Let us assume that Rev. Van Gelizer's church elects to set aside $270 each month for the pastor, having selected a combination of investments, life insurance, and income continuation in the event of his disability. Assuming Rev. Van Gelizer's age to be forty-five and the agreement to be funded until he becomes sixty-five, the plan could look like this: The board buys whole life insurance on Rev. Van Gelizer ($25,000 insurance—fully paid at age sixty-five) with a disability waiver of premium. So, in the event of his death, the board has $25,000 to assist his family; in the event of his disability, the insurance premium stops, but the protection and cash values continue as if the premiums were being paid. The board also purchases a disability policy that will pay Rev. Van Gelizer $500 per month until he is sixty-five in the event of his disability, thus taking the burden off the church. The $500 a month, when added to Social Security disability benefits, would provide an income to Rev. Van Gelizer and his family. The board then invests the remaining amount in Certificates of Deposit or other conservative investments. At age sixty-five there will be a fund of over $100,000 (compounding at 7 percent). This fund has grown tax free and has been invested with before-tax dollars.

At retirement, if Rev. Van Gelizer asked the church to purchase an annuity with the retirement fund, the board could buy, at today's rates, an annuity that would give him about $900 per month for the rest of his life, with at least ten years certain. The annuity income, added to his Social Security benefits, should see the pastor and his wife through retirement quite well. The best part is much of the money was donated by Uncle Sam.

Income Tax Differences

Let's look at the income tax difference between Pastor Savem and Rev. Van Gelizer.

Savem	Van Gelizer
Gross Pay . . . $1500	Gross Pay . . . $1230

From Pastor Savem's gross pay we must subtract $200 savings, $30 life insurance, and approximately $90 for medical expense, or a total of $320 per month that he spends "after tax." We can see that Pastor Savem has an annual income of $18,000, from which he allows $3500 in Schedule C deductions. He then has a taxable income of $14,500 on which he must pay federal income tax of $1157, not including self-employment tax or state tax.

Now let's take a look at Rev. Van Gelizer's income of $14,760 (12 × $1230). Why does he only receive $1230 gross pay? Remember that the $270 the board is using to fund the deferred compensation agreement is not considered income until Rev. Van Gelizer receives it. He is not considered to have "constructive receipt" of the funds as long as they remain an asset of the church. We allow the same $3500 Schedule C deductions. Rev. Van Gelizer then has a taxable income of $11,260 on which he pays taxes of $578, which is $579 less than Pastor Savem pays. Yet Rev. Van Gelizer retires with an income in excess of Social Security, and Uncle Sam has donated over $500 each year to Rev. Van Gelizer's usable income. Wouldn't any board prefer to protect and help its pastor and at the same time show a better financial statement?

This illustration has been very general and should not be considered legal advice. It is hoped, however, that it will

encourage some pastors and boards to investigate the pos-
sibilities and consult competent attorneys and
accountants.

CHAPTER 6

Housing Allowances

The question of who qualifies for a housing allowance and the right and wrong ways to handle housing allowances are important issues faced by many in the ministry.

Who Qualifies?

Previously, we have seen clergymen as basically pastors of a flock. For the sake of housing allowances, we will broaden our scope to include ordained clergy (in some cases, licensed or commissioned) in all phases of the Lord's work. There are times when what seems logical and right will be looked upon as illogical by the IRS. For example, we may have a clergyman who is employed as a teacher or administrator by a school, college, or university. If the educational institution is under the authority of a religious body constituting a church or church denomination, the clergyman can qualify for the rental allowance exclusion. Under these stipulations he is regarded to be performing services in the exercise of his ministry. However, such is not the case if the ordained minister's specific duties do not involve ecclesiastical functions and/or the educational institution on whose faculty he is serving is not under the authority of a religious body. Then he cannot qualify and cannot exclude from his income either a housing allowance or the value of the home furnished to him.[1]

Those churches that designate religious workers as minister of music or minister of education must be aware that without the ordination and authorization to perform *all* of the ecclesiastical duties of a duly ordained minister of the gospel, those persons may not exclude from income a rental allowance or the value of a home furnished them.

Another special case that concerns rental allowances or parsonages furnished to the pastor occurs when Bible college or seminary students are used as part-time, interim pastors or assistant pastors. These students, unless they are duly ordained, may not exclude rental allowances; in the case of a furnished parsonage, they must show fair rental value as income.[2] As we have stated, the rules do not have to make sense; they just have to be kept.

How Much Is Allowed?

There also seems to be confusion on the part of many pastors and church administrators regarding the amount for housing or parsonage allowances. The question seems to be: "What may I include in the allowance?" The IRS has not put a ceiling on the amount that can be designated; however, the IRS takes the position that the allowance should not be higher than the fair rental value of the home, including the cost of providing furnishings, the cost of additions such as a garage, and utilities. Note that the IRS uses the words "fair rental value."

In some parts of the country, home prices have skyrocketed as a result of inflation and housing shortages. Some pastors, who own their own homes and have owned them for some time, have been advised to refinance their homes to the maximum loan as a means of reducing their taxable income. This, of course, increases the amount of the mortgage payment. I should warn pastors that the total cost of their new mortgage repayment may exceed the fair rental value, particularly when taxes and insurance are added. The parsonage or housing allowance was not, nor is it now, intended to be a gimmick to be used for profit. It was intended to help the pastor by relieving him of a tax burden, not to help him avoid taxes.

What Can Be Excluded?

A pastor may exclude from his gross income such housing expenses as:

1. Rent or mortgage payments, or a down payment on a new home;
2. Taxes and interest;
3. Insurance on his home and its contents;
4. Repairs and upkeep on his home;
5. Cost of furniture and appliances, and their repair;
6. Utilities, including trash pickup and cable TV; and
7. Gardening.[3]

It can be seen here that the allowance is without doubt one of the largest tax breaks pastors will ever be given. I pray that it won't be abused.

IRS regulations state that a duly ordained minister of the gospel may exclude from his gross income the rental value of a home (including utilities) furnished to him as part of his compensation or the rental allowance paid to him as part of his compensation to the extent that such allowance is used by him to rent or otherwise provide a home. However, he must use the allowance in the year it was received to provide a home or pay utilities for a home furnished to him. Here is the part I find most often neglected. The clergyman receives the benefit of exemption only if the church or organization which employs him officially designates the payment as a rental allowance *before* the payment is made. A resolution by an executive committee of a national church agency is not sufficient to designate a rental allowance for ministers who are paid by a local congregation. The local congregation must officially designate that part of his compensation as rental allowance; if no part is officially designated as such, then the entire salary is includable in the clergyman's income.[4]

Contract of Employment

In my opinion, every clergyman should have a contract of employment, but not because of potential disagreements between the board and the pastor. The contract could help the pastor avoid potential problems if and when he is audited by the IRS. As a minister he is considered to be self-employed and thus must file a Schedule C (Profit or [Loss] from Business or Profession) of Form 1040 (see Appendix).[5] Because he is considered to be a professional, his professional expenses are deductible when they are "ordinary and necessary" to the successful completion of his profession.[6] In an audit he should be prepared to show that each area of expense is ordinary in the work of the ministry and necessary to its fulfillment.

One of the reasons I am in favor of contracts of employment for pastors is that most auditors are not knowledgeable regarding the ministry and what it involves. Their opinion of what is "ordinary and necessary" most likely will not agree with that of a pastor. The auditor will have to be convinced that the expense as entered on the Schedule C is a common occurrence in the pastor's job and that his ministry would not have been as complete or successful without the expense. Remember, the auditor is used to seeing a Schedule C completed by a businessman or professional in a profit-making enterprise.

The pastor will have to show him that success in the ministry is not predicated on financial profit, but on the fulfilling of the call that God has put upon the clergyman's life. If the pastor has an employment agreement, it will spell out this call. It may say, for example: The pastor is to preach the gospel, administer the ordinances of the church, instruct the flock, strengthen the weak, give comfort to the hurting, and care for the needy.

The contract or employment agreement can and should spell out the housing allowance arrangements. If the pastor is questioned regarding these matters, the agreement, in most cases, will convince the auditors that the Schedule C expenses are legitimate and will prove his official designation regarding his housing allowance.

This, in my opinion, is the best and most ethical way to handle the housing allowance for all concerned, including the Treasury Department. In the event the local church does not wish to make an employment contract, the next best method would be a resolution which is entered in the minutes.

Church Affiliation

You will recall that a clergyman employed as a teacher or administrator of a school, which is under the authority of a church, can qualify for the housing allowance exclusion if he is an ordained minister and if he performs his functions as a clergyman. Remember though that a clergyman who performs the same function but is not under church affiliation may not qualify for the exclusion. This being the case, what about evangelists and other clergymen who are in the ministry but not affiliated with a church? I am sorry to say that a recent Revenue Ruling put many clergymen into a position of doubtful qualification for housing allowances. The new ruling seems to indicate that, unless the clergyman has church affiliation or is under the control of the church, he most likely will not qualify for the housing allowance exclusion (Revenue Ruling 78-172, IRB 1978-19.9).

CHAPTER NOTES

1. U.S., Department of the Treasury, *Taxable Income and Nontaxable Income*, IRS Publication 525, 1978, p. 9.

2. Ibid.

3. Ibid.

4. Ibid.

5. Over the last few years a great deal of confusion has come about as a result of a lack of consistency regarding whether or not a pastor is self-employed. The use of Schedule C is open to various opinions. Some believe that income should be reported on a W-2 form and the pastor should be considered a common law employee. Others think that income should be reported on a 1099 form and the pastor should be regarded as a self-employed individual.

    In 1980 the IRS issued Revenue Ruling 80-110 in an effort to clarify the tax reporting of ministers. This ruling did not attempt to address the question of the employment status of ministers. Rather, it presumed that the minister is an employee—in my opinion, a presumption that was neither called for nor accurate. Suffice it to say, if you as a pastor have been considered self-employed (i.e., use tax forms 1040-ES, Schedule C, and Schedule SE) and your income is reported on a 1099, I would ask you to consider carefully the merits of this before you request a change to employee status. If, in the past, you have been considered an employee by your organization, you might want to read any one of a number of books, particularly *Shepherd or Hireling?* In this work, the authors lend sound support for the self-employed status of ministers.

    One of the strongest arguments for the self-employed status of the minister is the precedent set over the past many years. Courts of law and legislative bodies pay close attention to precedent in the determination of a particular point of law or interpretation of law.

    It must be pointed out that if there is a wholesale switch by most ministers to the methodology suggested in Revenue Ruling 80-110, a new precedent could establish itself which could have the effect of solidifying an otherwise questionable procedure. Denominational leaders, clergy tax authors, and others to whom ministers listen may suggest compliance with this Revenue Ruling and actually enhance its status into a precedent. Thus may come to fulfillment that famous Pogo statement: "WE HAVE MET THE ENEMY AND HE IS US!" (*Shepherd or Hireling*?, Stephen C. Merriman and John M. Simon [Downey, Calif.: Clergy Tax & Financial Services, 1980], p. 30).

6. U.S., Department of the Treasury, *Federal Income Tax Forms and Instructions*, IRS Publication 1040, 1981, p. 31.

CHAPTER 7

Social Security

Another area of confusion exists that is related to the pastor and Social Security. A large part of the confusion stems from the change in the Social Security Act as it relates to the clergy after 1967. For the sake of our discussion in this chapter, we will deal with post-1967 rulings and try to avoid any more confusion by not discussing any of the pre-1968 rules.

Self-Employment Tax

The first area of confusion for many people has been the dual name of Social Security coverage. It is important to know that self-employment tax, Social Security coverage, and FICA all mean the same thing. The term *Social Security coverage* is normally used when a person is an employee. For our purposes, we will use the term *self-employment tax*. The reason for our use of this term can be found in the language of IRS Publication 517.

> For social security purposes, you [a minister] compute your earnings from services as a member of the clergy as if you were self-employed, even though you may be performing those services as an employee.[1]

I have talked with pastors who have assured me that their churches are paying their self-employment tax. This may be true, but look at what the IRS says about that. Again I quote from Publication 517.

> If a church pays any amount toward your [a minister's] obligation for your income tax or self-employment tax other than from your salary, this is additional income to you and must be included in your gross income and self-employment income.[2]

Voluntary Withholding

It is also important to note that a minister's pay for service in the exercise of his ministry is not subject to income tax withholding. However, a minister may be able to enter into a voluntary withholding agreement with his employer to cover any income taxes he may have due.

A church's voluntary withholding of income taxes is covered by Internal Revenue Code Section 3402(p)(2). This section states that, for the purposes of Internal Revenue Code Chapter 24, "remuneration or other payments with respect to which such agreement is made shall be treated as if they were wages paid by an employer to an employee. . . ."

Tax Forms for the Clergyman

This is a good place to stress the forms required of an ordained minister in the exercise of his ministry. As an ordained minister, you are considered to be self-employed even though you work for a church or church organization. As a self-employed person, you are required to file income tax forms: 1040-ES (Declaration of Estimated Tax for Individuals), Schedule C (Profit [or Loss] from Business or Profession), and Schedule SE (Computation of Social Security Self-Employment Tax), in addition to your regular Form 1040 (see Appendix).

It would be wise for pastors to visit the local IRS office and pick up Publication 505 (*Tax Withholding and Esti-*

mated Tax). Many younger pastors may be surprised, particularly those in smaller, non-denominational churches; few seem to be aware that a clergyman must file a declaration of estimated tax on Form 1040-ES. He must pay the estimated tax or at least the first installment on or before April 15 of any year in which he expects to owe income tax and/or self-employment tax of $100 or more. If he is abroad on April 15, the filing date is automatically extended to June 15.[3]

To Be Exempt from Social Security

Recently, a young pastor visited my office for some advice regarding his personal finances. In the course of our conversation, he informed me that he was not going to pay any Social Security. He had been advised that he could send in a form and not have to pay it. He also was told that all that he had paid to Social Security in the past could be "frozen" and thus be available to him at a later date.

Let's look at the facts, as viewed by the IRS in Publication 517.

> The earnings that you receive as a member of the clergy are automatically covered and are subject to self-employment tax unless you are a member of a religious order and have taken a vow of poverty, or unless you request and receive from the Internal Revenue Service an exemption on religious grounds that you are opposed, by reason of conscience or religious principles, to accepting social security benefits . . . based on your services as a member of the clergy. Members . . . who file Form 4361 claiming exemption from social security coverage solely for economic considerations have not made a valid election and must pay self-employment tax.[4]

The opposition need not be to the acceptance of all public insurance, only to the acceptance of payments which are based on services performed as a minister. Thus, a clergyman may still be eligible for exemption, even though he isn't opposed to Social Security benefits with respect to services he performed outside the exercise of his ministry. We can see that the young man could have filed Form 4361 and excluded himself from Social Security on his earnings as a minister, and yet could pay Social Security on any earnings from any other job he might have at any time.

I am sure there are circumstances where the exemption would be appropriate, but in this case, the young man just did not want to pay the self-employment tax because he was convinced the system would not be in operation when he was old enough to collect. As we have seen, the exemption is not valid if the objection is for any reason other than "conscience or religious principles."

There is another reason for reading Form 4361 closely (see Appendix). In Section J of the instructions, it states: "You may not revoke the exemption once it is received."[5] Also, you need to be aware that Form 4361 cannot be filed later than two years after you have received earnings of $400 or more per year as a clergyman.

Benefits for Survivors

Many look at Social Security simply as retirement benefits, when in reality the best area of protection is the benefit paid to survivors (i.e., the pastor's wife and children in the event of his death). For example, let us take a typical pastor, forty-five years old, who has two children. Let's assume his children are ages twelve and fourteen, and his wife is age forty. We will estimate a conservative 3 percent inflation rate per year for the next twenty years.

In the event the pastor dies and is sufficiently covered by Social Security, what can his family expect in the way of benefits? His family should receive a lump sum payment at his death of $255, and Mrs. Pastor can expect an approximate average of $793 a month until the oldest child is eighteen years of age. Then, while the youngest child is still under eighteen, she could expect approximately $750 a month. The income to Mrs. Pastor would stop when both children reach the age of eighteen. However, if the children remain unmarried and attend an accredited school, each child could expect to receive approximately $300 a month from age eighteen to twenty-two. These dollars would go directly to them, not to Mrs. Pastor. After her youngest child reaches age eighteen, Mrs. Pastor is in what is called the "blackout period." This simply means that she will not be entitled to any Social Security benefit until she is age sixty; in this case, that would be fourteen years. From age sixty on, she should receive an average of $1200 a month. Remember, we have been inflating the projected benefit at 3 percent, and Social Security benefits could be changed by law.

Check Your Account

From the above illustration, we can see that Social Security is not just a retirement plan but a very valuable protection to the pastor's family in the event of his death. Since the protection available to your family is so important, it is wise to verify that the Department of Health, Education, and Welfare (Social Security Administration) is correct in its record keeping for your account. Their own form letter stresses:

> Unless you report an error within 3 years, 3 months, and 15 days after the year in which the wages were paid or after the taxable year in which the self-employment income was derived, correction of our records may not be possible.[6]

To check on your records and status, simply write: Social Security Administration, P.O. Box 57, Baltimore, MD

21203. Indicate your Social Security number and your date of birth, along with your name (as it appears on your card) and address. Ask for a statement of earnings and the number of quarters of coverage you have now. It would be wise to do this every three years to avoid possible problems at your retirement, death, or disability.

Disability Benefits

Now, what about Social Security disability benefits? The first thing you should be aware of is that Social Security benefits are not guaranteed as they relate to disability or any other benefit. The benefit may be lost in several ways. Let us take the language directly from the U.S. Department of Health, Education, and Welfare booklet *Your Social Security*.

> Under social security, you're considered disabled if you have a severe physical or mental condition which: Prevents you from working, and Is expected to last (or has lasted) for at least 12 months, or Is expected to result in death. Your checks can start for the 6th full month of your disability. Once checks start, they'll continue as long as you are disabled. If you are severely disabled, you could get benefits even though you manage to work a little.[7]

If a pastor who has not elected exemption from Social Security becomes disabled and he is not able to work in any substantially gainful job, and if he meets the work credits criteria, he will receive disability income after six months of his disability. Of course, the amount of income will be reduced if the pastor receives workers' compensation or if he is able to earn money.

Let me define work credits for disability benefits. If you become disabled before you are age twenty-four, you need credit for 1½ years of work in the three years before you become disabled. If you are between ages twenty-four and thirty-one, you must have credit for half the time between your twenty-first birthday and the date you become disabled. If you become disabled after age thirty-one, you need as much credit as you would need if you reached retirement age in the year you were disabled. Five years of your work must be in the ten-year period just before you became disabled. If you become disabled by blindness, the work requirement is somewhat different. You still need as much credit, but you do not need to meet the recent work requirements. It might be wise, at this point, to become familiar with some of the terms used in measuring insurability.

- If a person is insured at all, he or she is either "currently insured" or "fully insured" or both. It depends on the "quarters of coverage" credited.

- *Quarter of coverage.* A calendar quarter in which at least $50 in wages is paid to a worker, or any and all quarters in a year for which at least $400 of self-employment income is received. . . .

- *Currently insured.* A status of *limited* eligibility that provides family death benefits only; does not provide old-age or disability benefits. To qualify as currently insured a worker need have only 6 quarters of coverage in the 13-quarter period ending with the period in which he or she dies. . . .

- *Fully insured.* A status of *complete* eligibility that provides benefits in the event the worker dies . . . or reaches retirement age . . . or becomes disabled. . . . To qualify as fully insured, a person must have: (1) One quarter of coverage . . . for each calendar year that has elapsed after 1950, or after . . . he or she attains age 21, . . . up to the calendar year in which he or she dies, reaches age 62 after 1974, or becomes disabled, or (2) 40 or more quarters of coverage.[8]

To attempt to outline the amounts you or your family might receive at a given time would take pages.

It would be wise for every pastor, regardless of his age, to visit a Social Security office. He could pick up some of the free booklets regarding benefit payments, not only for his own information but for others in his congregation.

CHAPTER NOTES

1. U.S., Department of the Treasury, *Social Security for Members of the Clergy and Religious Workers*, IRS Publication 517, 1978, p. 4.

2. Ibid., p. 3.

3. U.S., Department of the Treasury, *Tax Withholding and Estimated Tax*, IRS Publication 505, rev. November 1980, pp. 13, 16.

4. IRS Publication 517, p. 1.

5. U.S., Department of the Treasury, *Application for Exemption from Self-Employment Tax for Use by Ministers, Members of Religious Orders and Christian Science Practitioners*, IRS Form 4361, rev. May 1980.

6. U.S., Department of Health, Education, and Welfare, Social Security Administration Form Letter OAR-7014a.

7. U.S., Department of Health, Education, and Welfare, *Your Social Security*, SSA Publication 79-10035, June 1979, p. 7.

8. *Social Security at-a-Glance* (Indianapolis: The Research and Review Service of America, Inc., June 1977), Index no. 3200.04.

CHAPTER 8

Taxes and Records

The single largest error that I have observed among attorneys, accountants, and their corporate clients (profit and nonprofit) is the assumption that once the corporate seal is obtained, little or no future maintenance is necessary to preserve the corporate integrity. The failure to maintain periodic corporate minutes reflecting corporate activity throughout the year, as well as minutes for the appropriate meetings of the board of directors, can result in serious difficulties for the corporation faced with an inquiry by the IRS or a lawsuit by a creditor.

Corporate Documentation

There are also reporting requirements and various enabling minutes needed with respect to insurance, pensions, salaries, leases, and contracts of employment. In other words, it is important that all necessary corporate activity be documented. How can a pastor stay on top of every aspect of corporate business? One of the best ways is to have an attorney on the board! This is not always possible. So, good record keeping by a competent secretary is important.

Let us assume that you do have an attorney who has helped you in your corporate affairs. (If you don't have an attorney, you would be well advised to find one.) Always send him all documents you receive from the:

1. Internal Revenue Service,

2. Secretary of State,
3. Administrator of any pension plan or trust, and
4. Government tax agencies—local, state, or federal.

If your board prepares any forms, a copy should be sent to your attorney. There are also a number of other areas for which your attorney should be consulted for legal advice or assistance. The following are of particular importance for his review:

1. Employment contracts,
2. Any contract before it is signed,
3. Employee workers' compensation injury, and
4. Any aspect of indebtedness—bonds, notes, and trusts.

It is imperative that your attorney be informed if there has been any change of address or changes in your board of directors or officers.

Financial Record Keeping

While accurate record keeping certainly includes the recording of minutes and corporate resolutions, it also involves detailed financial records. It is not the intent of this book to make an attorney or an accountant out of the pastor or the business manager. It is, however, very important that all those involved in the business of the corporation understand the importance of doing things in the right way (". . . Then He said to them, 'Then render to Caesar the things that are Caesar's; and to God the things that are God's' " Matthew 22:21).

Most people find it a bother to keep their financial records in order. Many tax men believe that the biggest mistake made is failure to keep accurate records of deductions and expenses. Tax record keeping is the highest paying job a minister will ever have. It has been estimated that ministers can save over $60 in taxes for every hour spent in careful record keeping.

Travel Expense

I have talked with a number of pastors who spend a great deal of time on the road. Many of these pastors keep very good records of their travel expenses, but some just aren't inclined to record their costs. They estimate what they spend and just deduct it on their tax returns. After all, they are "not about to cheat and, if anything, estimate low." Well, pastor, your testimony as to what you spend traveling to another city is not sufficient to support a deduction of travel expense. By law, your personal claim must be supported by other evidence—your records. Failure to keep adequate records usually will result in a disallowance of your travel expense deduction when there is an examination of your return.

What kind of records should you keep? When you travel, it is wise to keep two types of records. First, you should have a diary or appointment book showing the date, destination, and purpose of the trip. Second, you should keep detailed account of your expenses (i.e., travel, telephone, parking, taxi or car rental, meals, and business entertainment). When you have these expenses entered in your diary, remember that when your lodging, travel, or entertainment expenses exceed $25, you will need an itemized paid bill or receipt. A cancelled check by itself is not acceptable as proof.

Some pastors travel with their wives, and the question is often asked, "Can I deduct the cost of taking my wife?" Sometimes the answer is yes, and sometimes no! The circumstances will dictate the correct answer. If your wife accompanies you because you are lonesome and she has no other responsibilities while traveling with you, you cannot deduct her share of the expenses (so what!—take her anyway). If, however, she is important to the business at hand and is, in fact, important to the meeting, then, yes, her portion is deductible (see the goodwill entertainment test in a tax guide such as the *Research Institute of America* or the *Commerce Clearing House*).

Let me stress again that it is not the purpose of this chapter to make tax experts out of pastors nor is it to detract in any way from the importance of having qualified tax advisers. It is, however, my intent to alert you to some of the areas that are important and to help you see that they are handled correctly.

Auto Expense

No one enjoys keeping a constant record of miles traveled in pursuit of his ministry. It is, however, an absolute necessity. If you are audited and have not kept a mileage log, you will put your auto expense deduction in jeopardy.

There are two methods for computing your auto costs for tax purposes. You would be well advised to compute the cost both ways and choose the method that gives you the greatest deduction. The first method allows you to deduct a given number of cents for each mile driven for the purposes of your ministry. You also may deduct your actual cost for parking, tolls, and related expenses, in addition to the cents-per-mile. A daily log of miles driven should be kept and can be used for substantiation in the event of an audit.

The second method is more detailed in respect to record keeping. You would maintain an itemized list of your actual auto expenses such as gas, oil, lubrication, repairs, parts, insurance, and license. A large part of the expense is depreciation of your auto. In this second method, your record keeping must be detailed, and you must subtract the cost of personal driving and commuting to the office. Developing the habit of keeping records that will allow you to compute your actual auto expenses and of recording your professional miles will allow you to determine which method will give you the greater deduction. One last thought regarding auto expense: If you purchase an automobile for use in the ministry, you will want to discuss it with your tax adviser so that he can compute any investment tax credit that may be utilized.

Professional Expenses

All too often pastors do not keep adequate records of the money they spend for books, magazines, tapes, and newspapers. Books, as well as periodicals and newspapers, that are purchased for professional purposes are deductible in the year of purchase. If, however, you purchase major reference volumes, you will want to depreciate them over the useful life of the books (usually five to seven years). When you were ordained or entered into the professional ministry, you probably had a personal library. That library is now your professional library and may be depreciated at its fair market value established at the time you entered the ministry.

Office Supplies and Expenses

The office area in the home will not be discussed in this chapter. You should discuss this subject with your tax man. A word of caution: If you are receiving a housing allowance, you will not be entitled to an office-in-the-home deduction. However, you still will be allowed to deduct the expense of office supplies used in your ministry. The same can be said of office equipment, but if the equipment has a useful life of more than one year, it should be depreciated over its life expectancy.

The first thing a pastor should do, if he has not already done so, is to spend time inventorying his library, office equipment, and furnishings. This will accomplish two things. First, it would be necessary in the event of fire or theft. Second, it would help him begin record keeping that might prove valuable in the event of an audit.

Educational Expense

A common expense for ministers is that of continuing education for the development of skills in areas related to the ministry. In this complex world we find that pastors must have knowledge in areas that few would have imagined a few years ago. This book would not have been necessary in the early part of this century. Pastors are now expected to take classes in counseling, business administration, and so forth.

Since pastors are considered to be self-employed, they may deduct the expenses for continuing education on the Schedule C. Many taxpayers itemize such expenses on Schedule A of Form 1040. However, by deducting them on your Schedule C instead, you would lower your Social Security tax base and you would receive a greater benefit from the deduction.

Remember, though, that the education expense deduction must meet certain guidelines (i.e., the education must be incurred for the purpose of maintaining or improving your present job or professional skills). The deduction will not be allowed if the education qualifies you for a new trade or business. You, as a pastor, may not take a course in chemistry and deduct the cost of the course.

If the education does qualify, what may be deducted? Deductible expenses include tuition, books, supplies, fees, and transportation to school. If you must be away from home overnight, you may deduct meals and lodging.

To summarize, taxation is becoming more complex, and you as a pastor were not called to be a tax expert. The best advice I can give you is to keep good records, document everything, and find a competent tax adviser to assist you in your tax preparation. You will appreciate the need for adequate record keeping when the man from the Treasury Department knocks.

CHAPTER 9

The Pastor as an Executive

When pastors go to seminary, they learn that on the seventh day God ceased from all His work. When they become the leader of a flock, they suspect that on the seventh day God must have created staff meetings.

Staff Meetings

Staff meetings, like committee meetings, can be a source of great irritation to pastors and their staff. However, the staff meeting is a necessary means of effective *communication* and *management*, and it should serve both functions. Why, then, do so many staff meetings fall flat? Most of the time, the failure of the staff meeting to accomplish its purpose lies with the pastor or staff leader who has called the meeting.

There are a number of reasons why staff meetings create problems. Let's look at some of the reasons:

1. The meetings are held on a regular schedule even when there is nothing to be discussed.
2. The staff members have not done their homework, and the result is digression and disorganization.
3. The person-in-charge does not know how to conduct a meeting.
4. The meetings are held in an atmosphere or environment that is not conducive to a good discussion.
5. The meetings last too long.
6. Worst of all, the meetings do not start on time.

We have looked at some reasons why the meetings are not successful. Now, what can be done to correct the problem? There is no way to insure successful staff meetings, but some general principles should be followed.

1. Hold staff meetings regularly but not more often than is needed for worthwhile communication.
2. Don't let anyone monopolize the time. Balance the program. Establish give and take.
3. Put the decisions made in the meeting into practice. Make the meeting part of a vital system.
4. Have established objectives.
5. Be prepared.
6. Have someone in charge who is competent (but not always the pastor).

Pastor, it is your responsibility to be a Monday morning quarterback. You should determine through feedback whether the meeting really did achieve what you wanted. If you are not happy with staff meetings, if they are falling flat, try putting someone else in charge. Give your ego a rest.

It might be well for us to remember Paul's charge to those in Rome: ". . . I say to every man among you not to think more highly of himself than he ought to think; but to think so as to have sound judgment, as God has allotted to each a measure of faith" (Romans 12:3). There are those who have the ability to speak out in a group, and sometimes they will dominate through force of personality. Their strong natures or quick tongues often inhibit others in the group. I have found that it takes careful observation to draw out a good thought or a new idea from a more reticent staff member. In most cases, the least likely person can do a great job of leading a staff meeting when he is given a chance.

Management

If communication and management are the primary functions of staff meetings, it is important that we understand the terms. Because communication is such an everyday aspect of the pastor's job, we will not dwell on it. We will look at management very closely though. We will discuss the five basic functions of management:

1. Planning,
2. Organizing,
3. Staffing,
4. Controlling, and
5. Directing.

With these in mind, let us examine each one.

Prayer and Planning

Just as the pastor must set aside time for prayer, he also must set aside time for planning. It is not possible to "plan when I have time." The life of the church depends upon the two P's: prayer and planning. Prayer, without a doubt, is the single most important factor in any church's success, and through prayer comes the ability to plan creatively. It is as reasonable for a pastor to lock his office door, unplug the telephone, and plan as it is for him to go into his "closet" for prayer. There is no other way. You must set aside the time.

The springboard function of management is planning. Without it, things just happen; they "occur without apparent reason or design."[1] Effective planning makes demands on those who would be planners; time must be set aside for creative thought.

One of the greatest deterrents to planning is the urgent. In the course of an average day, a pastor or church leader may be called upon to extinguish many fires of varying intensities, some of which recur the next day. The more common varieties of urgencies are mediating and arbitrating misunderstandings; attending committee or staff meetings; counseling on the telephone; and responding to letters, all of which are important. However, one can fill an entire day with routine and mundane activities, and at the end of the day he will be exhausted. Yet, he will not possess any feeling of real accomplishment. The need to do the urgent can be compared to Gresham's law of monetary economics: Bad money drives out good money.[2] In other words, if one allows it, the day-to-day programmed and routine tasks can drive out the creative planning processes. Perhaps opportunities for growth may go unnoticed, be shoved aside, or be passed by entirely.

After you have set aside time for creative planning, the next step is understanding the two facets of planning. The first is short-range planning or problem solving. Some call this goal setting. As important as short-range planning is, it should be placed within the broader and, in my opinion, more important area of long-range planning.

The best definition of long-range planning is a description of an attempt to uncover God's strategy and to become a part of it. Short-range planning generally deals with a time span of one month to three years, and long-range planning looks beyond three years, out as far as ten or twenty years.

No one knows what tomorrow will bring. Certainly we cannot presume to know what is going to happen in ten years; however, we can know about today. What we do today will affect our tomorrows. The long-range planning we do will help us to understand the direction we are heading, so that the decisions we make today will be more appropriate in view of the future.

Don't consider the job of long-range planning completed after you have made your initial plans. The plans need to be reviewed and rewritten on a regular basis. Certainly the planning will need to be reconsidered and modifed at least annually.

At this point we might ask ourselves the question: Do we as Christians need to "go through" all this executive stuff, do we need to dwell on planning? Can't we just give it all to the Lord? Is all of this really Christian? The Bible has much to say on the subject of management; the word *steward* basically means manager. We have all been charged to be good managers of what God has given us. Dare we take management lightly? We know we cannot control the future, but we can plan toward a future, the kind of future that we believe God would have us live. Consider Proverbs 2:15: "The plans of the diligent lead surely to advantage, But everyone who is hasty comes surely to poverty." It certainly can be said that God had long-range plans; we know that from our reading of Genesis. He created the best plan of all: the plan of salvation.

Organizing and Staffing

For effective management, the next functions are organizing and staffing. Cohesiveness should be a prime goal of your organization. All departments must function as a part of the whole; all of the parts are equally important and make up the whole (1 Corinthians 12:12-14). The Apostle Paul has given us the guidelines; they are certainly as true today as they were when he wrote them.

However, each individual within your organization has talents unique to him or her. Your job is to put the right person in the right job. Often I have called upon a pastor and have been greeted by a receptionist who, though she was a lovely person, just did not have the right personality for the job. Remember, for many people the receptionist is the first, and sometimes the last, contact they will have with your church.

Select the right person for every one of the functions of your organization. Each individual must be able to perform with all the skill required for his position. Too often we have made do with mediocrity or worse; then we have overworked the able staff, while we put up with the unqualified. God's work deserves better.

Perhaps it is time to take a lesson from the world of business in this area. The competent executive knows that high caliber personnel do not usually come at bargain rates. It is not economical to hire people who perform on a mediocre level. In the world of business, Andrew Carnegie was without question a success. It is said that on his tombstone there is an inscription that reads, "I managed to hire men better than myself."

I am convinced that it is better to have one adequately paid, efficient, able person than any number of less capable ones. Most church boards consist of businessmen. If they are successful, they did not get there by accident. They had qualified people on their staff. Shouldn't you?

Now that you have dedicated, quality people, how do you retain them?

1. Give them a challenge.
2. Let them have responsibility.
3. Involve them in planning decisions.
4. Regard them as associates rather than subordinates.
5. Provide the opportunity for promotion from within the organization.

In short, weld them into a cohesive body. The "one-man-show" concept of leadership is neither scriptural nor conducive to morale or growth. Pastors should be careful, as Peter said, " . . . nor yet as lording it over those allotted to your charge . . . " (1 Peter 5:3). Pastors, in other words, should not be church bosses.

We all can read in the Bible about the pastor's role. We know the position the Lord took regarding bossism: "You know that those who are recognized as rulers of the Gentiles lord it over them. But it is not so among you . . . " (Mark 10:42,43). We must not confuse the role of leadership with authority just because of the call God has extended to pastors. There should be no confusion either that the flock willingly gave the pastor part of the authority that belonged to them. They give the authority to the pastor, and he dares not demand it. When authority or the "one-man-show" is excessive, it stifles communication and incentive. It also creates a feeling in staff members of "us" and "them" and a possibility of division within the organization.

I have seen the "one-man-show" situation carried to many extremes. Perhaps the most ludicrous is a pastor who spends precious time personally approving all of the checks for payroll and accounts payable. He thinks that this allows him to exercise his high position and indispensability. In reality, if the checks need to be written, the obligations already have been incurred and it is too late to approve or disapprove.

Staffing is the systematic involvement of people within the organization to accomplish the purpose of the organization. People are the primary resource of your church or organization.

Part of staffing is obviously recruiting. Your church or organization must put thought and effort into the task of recruiting or staffing. You need a method of recruiting rather than a last-minute "who-can-we-get-for-the-job" attitude. Too often the pastor or leader is carrying too much of the load. The board might decide that he needs an assistant. Finding the pastor an assistant will surely help the pastor, but is it going to solve the problem? Many organizations would do better to obtain a competent recruiter who also can function as a trainer. In this way, instead of just helping the pastor, the potential is there to multiply the ministry. Of course, the recruiter needs to be someone who shares the pastor's vision and knows the people who are available.

Often we find that those responsible for recruiting view the church or organization as a vehicle which uses people. However, they should view the church as a place where people relate to one another and perform tasks. It is imperative that we stop forcing people into jobs they don't want or for which they are not equipped. How often have you found that people who accepted a job after being pressured into it did not perform it well? Did they also complain so much that others caught the negative attitude?

We must remember that a Christian organization is unique in that we are all part of one another and we are responsible for one another. At the heart of every organization, Christian or otherwise, are the people. We, as Christians, must function with as much efficiency, if not more, than the world does. We also must set an example of unity. It is important that each member of the staff be able to identify with and strive toward the goals of the organization as a whole. Involvement in the organization's goals is a complete necessity no matter how small the task might be.

Controlling

Controlling and planning are almost twins. In planning you and your staff outline what you are going to do. In controlling you review the performance of the organization on a regular basis. You monitor and verify your immediate goal. Once your organization has reached its immediate goal, you must reevaluate your position and set new goals; the process of planning starts all over again. Remember, we all have one ultimate goal of serving Christ, and we must set ourselves toward that goal continually.

Directing

Directing an organization demands the qualities of leadership. If a pastor has truly been called by God to the ministry, he will have these qualities. Now he must begin to use these qualities in directing the organization. Directing begins with a clearly identified goal: one that is realistic and has the enthusiastic participation and support of everyone in the organization.

It is important in directing an organization to be specific about goals. Too often they are ill defined and the staff is left to guess How high is up? or How much is too many? Goals should be, when possible, quantified—such as dollars and cents, ratios, and time periods. This is not meant to imply that goals must be rigid. It is good practice to remain flexible enough to accomplish the goal rather than to set a rigid goal that is unattainable. If we keep in mind that all of our goals and plans are predicated upon the will of the Lord, we can say,

> Come now, you who say, "Today or tomorrow, we shall go to such and such a city, and spend a year there and engage in business and make a profit." Yet you do not know what your life will be like tomorrow. You are just a vapor that appears for a little while and then vanishes away. Instead, you ought to say, "If the Lord wills, we shall live and do this or that" (James 4:13-15).

Directing is in no way the same as dictating. People

must be permitted to apply their own thought processes and work habits to their jobs without feeling compelled to "obey or else." Individualism and latitude usually stimulate effectiveness and pride in work.

As we discussed in our section on planning, we should not allow solving problems to crowd out time for planning. So, what is the best way to go about problem solving? Here are a few techniques that have worked for many people over the years. Perhaps you will want to try them.

First and foremost, pray and then pray some more. Then, with God's help, start work on solving the problem. First, put the problem down on paper, put it into words. It is next to impossible to analyze a problem while it is only in your head. Get it out! Putting the problem down on paper forces you to be specific.

When you have it written down, ask yourself, "How can I solve this problem?" You must assume that there is a good solution. However, there are times when the only solution is to accept the situation for the present, and then not let it distract you from other important tasks. It is a profitable habit to distinguish between problems you can solve and those you cannot. If the problem seems to be one you should be able to solve, but you don't seem to be solving it, it could be that you have not identified the real problem.

Keep reviewing the specifics until you identify the real problem. Ask yourself, "What is the best possible way for me to solve this problem today?" In other words, focus your attention on the present. If you don't carry over assumptions from the past, you may gain fresh insight. Yesterday you might have used a technique for solving it that didn't work. If so, don't dwell on it—look for a new approach today.

When you approach a difficult situation, it is important to remember that the solution comes from only two sources: (1) information you have in your memory, and (2) new information obtained from other sources. Often information from memory alone is not enough. First, ask yourself, "How much do I know about the situation, and how and where can I obtain more information about it?" An active search for more than one way to understand the problem will increase the number of alternative solutions.

Not long ago I was following my own advice. I had outlined a situation on paper, and I had determined that I could solve the problem. I was at the point of finding the solution, when a long and perplexing telephone conversation interrupted my problem-solving time. When I got back to the problem, the solution seemed very distant. I had discovered that proper timing is important to solving many problems. Ask yourself, "Is this the best time to work out the solution?" If it is not, move on to something else, if possible. You might even find, as I did, that the problem was not nearly as large or as perplexing the next day.

I might as well confess that what I was concerned about was a "people problem"; it involved my opinion versus another's in a particular situation. The next day I was able to see that if I gave my ego a rest and let the other person be right, when in fact we both were a little right and a little wrong, the problem could be solved.

I read recently that one of the biggest time wasters in the day-to-day functioning of an organization is the game of buck passing, blaming, and just plain needing to be right. Too often we view being wrong as a sign of failure and thus being right becomes all important. Often hurt feelings also accompany the proving that "I am right." One's need to be right all the time will intimidate people. People will feel it is a waste of time to discuss an issue with those who think they are always right or become offended if they are not right all the time. People will think, "He already has his mind made up," and a great deal of creative thinking and discussion will be stifled. Most of the time it is not a matter of right or wrong, just differences of opinion.

Beware though of the oversimplified answer. Sometimes our wish for a simple solution causes us to reject anything that appears slightly complicated. In this event we may fail to size up a situation accurately because we have oversimplified it. Some problems just do not have simple answers, and searching for simple solutions just will not work. The problem must be solved by pure hard work.

This brings us to the next-to-the-last of the problem-solving techniques. Sometimes we must stop looking for a perfect solution. Seldom have I found an absolutely perfect solution for any problem. Some of us fail to realize this. We do not want to try any solution unless it is certain to work. What we should do is try the most promising solution and continue to look for a better one. Even a mediocre solution, if used, is better than a superior one never put into action.

Now for the last, and best, problem-solving technique: give the Holy Spirit permission to work. How many times have you had what seemed to be an unsolvable problem, and after making desperate attempts to solve it, you have gone to bed only to awaken with an answer? Some credit the subconscious. I prefer to thank the Lord and give the credit to the Holy Spirit. Can we use this as a technique for problem solving? Certainly! Learn all you can about the problem, and then let your mind digest it. Pray about it. Give it to the Holy Spirit, and then try not to be surprised when the answer comes at a totally unexpected time.

I am certain that the above techniques will not solve all the problems the modern clergyman meets daily. It is my hope, however, that these suggestions might give you some new insights into problem solving.

CHAPTER NOTES

1. *Random House College Dictionary*, rev. ed., s.v. "happen."

2. Paul Dickson, *The Official Rules* (New York: Dell Publishing Co., Inc., 1978), p. 5.

CHAPTER 10

Are You Ready for the Audit Now?

We have seen some of the problems pastors face and some of the answers to the problems. We have looked at the "dangerous opportunity" or "crisis," and now we must learn from it. I have not tried to answer all the questions regarding the subjects we have discussed in the previous chapters. Rather, my intent has been to raise more questions. Until the clergy and church leaders become aware of the questions they need to ask, they will not solve any of the problems that are beginning to compound themselves.

Each year thousands of young men go into the ministry. For the most part they are ill equipped to handle the intricacies of corporate structure. Yet, in the last few years we have seen ministries of every type being used of the Lord: music ministries, theatrical ministries, and tape ministries. We know that in many cases the first step toward a newly formed ministry is the formation of a nonprofit corporation. We have viewed the challenge in two ways: without corporate structure; and with corporate structure, and its attendant problem of being a corporation-in-fact, not just in form. Both ways, corporate and non-corporate, present very real problems. In the non-corporate ministry, we found clergymen who could not receive tax-deductible contributions, and thus support for their ministries was hard to come by.

I am sorry to say that men going into the ministry think of a nonprofit corporate structure as simply a vehicle through which people may give on a deductible basis. In fact, however, the corporation is and should be a very viable part of the ministry. Some ministries, after obtaining nonprofit status, do not follow through and file an application for exemption. This can be a major mistake.

We also have examined some of the problems of personal record keeping: tax reporting, Social Security and self-employment tax, housing allowances, and employment contracts.

Other important topics such as putting your own house in order, estate planning, fund raising, deferred giving, and the use of tax law in trusts and annuities, have not even been touched. It would be impossible to include all those topics in the space we have. More importantly, they are areas of such complexity that you should seek specialized legal counsel regarding them.

Again, let me urge you to seek counsel on matters such as these. This is good stewardship. Don't think you can be all things to the ministry. You cannot be both spiritual leader and businessman. One or both areas are bound to suffer.

Until your organization can put a business manager on staff, *please* seek competent counsel from professionals. I have indicated that one of the most important people to your ministry is your accountant. Now let me stress again—your tax expert and your lawyer are parts of the vital team that make your ministry function as it should. Many will say, "We can't afford it." Yet, it seems to me that they cannot afford to be without good counsel.

The church must present a good witness to the world. Like it or not, we must know the law and adhere to it. For too long we have hidden our heads in the sand regarding our responsibilities in Section 501(c)(3) of the Internal Revenue Code. The time has come to be aware of what the law asks of us and what we can expect of it. If we understand and obey it, we might find the law to be on our side. If we do not "render unto Caesar what is Caesar's," I feel certain we are going to find the tax-exempt status of the church in crisis. It might be more correct to say that the exempt status of the church is already in crisis. In the *Fordham Law Review,* an article by Sharon L. Worthing sounds the alert.

IRS has greatly expanded its monitoring of tax-exempt organizations in the past decade. A centralized, highly developed system has been created which focuses particularly on organizations exempt under section 501(c)(3), the category which includes churches. Though churches are presently relieved from compulsory participation in the system, this relief has been challenged in Congress twice.

The current challenge to such relief is the recent Treasury definition of an integrated auxiliary of a church, which requires church-related organizations to file information returns. Though this requirement might seem to be of minor importance, it represents the formal induction of religious organizations as a class into compulsory IRS monitoring. This, in turn, raises questions about the constitutionality of having religious organizations under a program of government surveillance. The constitutional difficulty encountered is one of excessive government entanglement with religion.

Although the entanglement created by having church-related institutions file informational returns does not seem terribly great, the requirement can be seen as a first step whose ultimate end is full government surveillance of religious institutions. The excessive entanglement test serves as a "warning signal" regarding programs which may appear harmless, but whose ultimate expression would result in a clearly unconstitutional relationship between church and state. Judged in this light, expansion of the information return requirement to include church-related institutions results in an unconstitutional entanglement of government with religion.[1]

As you can see, Sharon L. Worthing feels that we already have an unconstitutional situation relating to government entanglement with religion. She is not alone in her thinking. The crisis is becoming more real every day. We must wake up to the reality of it.

In its evangelical enthusiasm, the Christian church sometimes has not given enough priority to learning the requirements of the law. Thus, it cannot present itself spotless and without blemish. In many cases, we may not agree with the IRS or the government decisions, and we may take issue with the law as it is. Still our responsibility is to adhere to the words of the Apostle Peter.

> Submit yourselves for the Lord's sake to every human institution, whether to a king as the one in authority, or to governors as sent by him for the punishment of evildoers and the praise of those who do right. For such is the will of God that by doing right you may silence the ignorance of foolish men (1 Peter 2:13-15).

CHAPTER NOTE

1. Sharon L. Worthing, "The Internal Revenue Service as a Monitor of Church Institutions: The Excessive Entanglement Problem," *Fordham Law Review* 45 (1977), pp. 947-948.

DEFINITION OF TERMS

Absolute Gift: A gift of property by will, which carries with it possession of and complete dominion over the property; opposite of conditional gift.

Abstract of Title: A summary of all essential facts relating to the title to a parcel of real property.

Accrual Basis of Accounting: Income is credited when the legal right to the income occurs, and expenses are charged when the legal liability becomes enforceable.

Accrued Interest: Interest that has been earned since the date of the last interest payment.

Accumulated Income: The amount of income from a trust which is retained in the account.

Acknowledgment: A declaration of an act or of a fact to give the act or fact legal validity.

Acquittance: A discharge of an obligor from his obligation.

Actuary: A person trained in the highly technical aspects of insurance, particularly in the mathematics of mortality tables and the calculations of premiums, reserves, and other values.

Adjudication: The decision of a competent court regarding matters in dispute.

Adjusted Gross Estate: The value of an estate for estate settlement purposes, after all allowable deductions have reduced the gross estate. Federal estate taxes are based upon the adjusted gross estate.

Administrator: The person appointed by a court to settle an estate, usually when there is no will. If the person is a woman, she is called an administratrix.

Administrator with the Will Annexed (Administrator C.T.A.): When a will names an executor to administer the estate, and the named executor either does not act or ceases to act before the estate is distributed, and no successor executor is named in the will, someone must be appointed to act. This person is called the administrator with the will annexed.

Administratrix: See administrator.

Adverse Possession: An occupation of land inconsistent with the right of the true owner.

Affiant: A person who makes an affidavit or settlement under oath or affirmation.

Affidavit: A document sworn to and signed before a notary or other court officer, which contains a specific statement.

Agent: A person who acts for another person called a principal by the latter's authority. The distinguishing characteristics of an agent are threefold: first, that he act on behalf and subject to the control of his principal; second, that he does not have title to the property of his principal; and third, that he owes the duty of obedience to his principal's orders.

Allocation: The crediting of a receipt in its entirety; the disbursing of funds in total to one account.

Amendment: An addition, deletion, or change in a legal document.

Amortization: The process in which a debt is liquidated by periodic payments to a creditor (i.e., the amount needed in periodic payments which will pay off the debt in a specific number of payments).

Ancillary: Subordinate or auxiliary to something or someone else.

Annual Report: The financial statement issued annually by a corporation to its stockholders.

Annuitant: A person who receives an annuity.

Annuity: A fixed amount (sometimes variable) of money payable periodically. It is paid either for the life of the annuitant or for a definite period of time.

Appraisal: The evaluation of property.

Appreciation: An increase in value of property; opposite of depreciation.

Arbitrage: The buying of stocks, bonds, or other securities in one market and selling in another.

Assets: Everything a corporation owns, including cash, equipment, furnishings, investments, accounts due, materials, and inventories.

Assignee: A person appointed by another or by the court to do some act or enjoy some right, privilege, or property.

Assignment: The legal transfer of right or interests in property to another person.

Assignor: A person who makes a transfer of title or interest in writing.

Attest: To serve as a witness to; as to attest a will or other document.

Attorney in Fact: A person who, acting as an agent, has been given written authorization by another person to transact business for him out of court.

Balance Sheet: A tabular statement of both sides of a set of accounts in which the debit and credit balances add up as equal; a statement of the financial position of a business on a specified date.

Beneficiary: The person named in an insurance policy or will (trust) to receive property and/or money.

Bequeath: To give personal property by will; to be distinguished from *devise,* dealing with real property.

Bequest: A gift of personal property by will.

Bid and Asked: A quotation of the best price which will be paid and the lowest priced offering of a security at a given moment.

Bonafide: In good faith (e.g., a bonafide offer).

Bond: A formal written obligation whereby the maker agrees to pay money either absolutely or upon certain conditions.

Book Value: The stated sum of all of a company's assets, minus its liabilities, divided by the number of common shares outstanding is the book value per common share.

Buy-Sell Agreement: An agreement wherein the owners of a business arrange to transfer their respective ownership interests upon the death of one, or upon some other event, so as to provide continued control of the business or some other desired end.

Capital Gain or Loss: Profit or loss from the sale of an asset, recognized by the tax laws as differing in kind from profit or loss from the asset's use.

Capital Stock: The total amount of stock, common and preferred, that a corporation is authorized to issue under its certificate or incorporation or charter.

Cash Basis: An accounting method in which income is not credited for income tax until it is received and expenses are not charged until they have been paid.

Cash Surrender Value: The cash value of a life insurance policy, if redeemed before the death of the insured.

Charitable Bequest: A gift of personal property to a legal charity by will.

Charitable Remainder: An arrangement wherein the remainder interest goes to charity upon the termination or failure of a prior interest.

Charitable Trust: A trust created for the benefit of a legal charity.

Charity: An agency, institution, or organization in existence and operated for the benefit of an indefinite number of persons and conducted for education, religious, scientific, medical, or other beneficient purpose.

Closed Corporation: One whose entire stock is held by one person or by a few persons; not public.

Codicil: The only legal document which can change a will. An amendment or supplement to a will executed with the same formalities as a will.

Collateral: Specific property, commonly securities, given by a borrower to a lender as a pledge for the payment of a loan or other obligation.

Commingled Fund: A common fund in which the monies of several accounts are mixed.

Community Property: Property in which a husband and wife each have an undivided one-half interest by reason of marriage.

Conservator: An individual or trust institution appointed by a court to manage property.

Consideration: Something of value given by one party to another in exchange for the promise or act of such other party.

Contest of a Will: An attempt by legal process to prevent the probate of a will or the distribution of property according to the will.

Conveyance: The transfer of title to real property or the writing effecting the transfer of real property, such as a deed.

Corpus (Body): The principal or capital of an estate, as distinguished from the income.

Curtesy: The life estate of a widower in the real property of his wife.

Custodian: One whose duty it is to hold, safeguard, and account for property committed to his care.

Debenture: A promissory note secured only by the general credit and assets of a company and usually not backed by a mortgage or lien on any specific assets.

Decedent: A deceased person.

Declaration of Trust: An acknowledgment by one holding or taking title to property that he holds in trust for the benefit of someone else, usually made in writing.

Decree: The decision of a court of equity, admiralty, probate, or divorce; as distinguished from judgment of a court of law.

Deed: Written instrument, signed, sealed, and delivered according to the applicable law, containing some transfer, bargain, or contract with respect to property.

Default: The failure to make a payment when due, regarding a bond or promissory note.

Deferred Income: Income deferred until a time in the future when earned income is lower; thus income tax liability is potentially less.

Deficiency Judgment: A judgment for the balance of a debt after the security has been exhausted.

Demand Note: A promissory note payable on demand.

Demise: Death.

Depletion: An allowance given to companies in the natural resource industries to compensate for the fact that the resources they are exploiting will eventually be exhausted.

Deposition: A written testimony of a witness under oath, before a qualified officer of the court, to be used in place of his oral testimony at a trial or other hearing.

Depreciation: A decrease in value; opposite of appreciation.

Devise: A gift of real property by will.

Disclaimer: A denial of any interest in or claim to the subject of action (i.e., renunciation of any title or interest).

Dissent: The act of disagreeing.

Divest: To annul or take away a vested right.

Dividend: A payment authorized by a board of directors in cash or in stock; usually a distribution made from current or past profits. A dividend is not a deductible expense to a corporation.

Donee: One who receives a gift.

Donor: One who makes a gift.

Dower: The life estate of a widow in real property of her husband.

Encumbrance: Any right to or interest in real property which lowers its value but does not prevent its transfer, subject to the encumbrance.

Endorsement: A writing, usually the name of the payee, on the deck (the back) of a negotiable instrument, whereby the property represented by the instrument is transferred.

Estate: All property, real and personal, tangible and intangible, in which a person has an interest.

Executor: The person named in a will to carry out its terms.

Fiscal Year: A corporation's accounting year. It need not coincide with the calendar year.

Grantee: Person to whom property is transferred by deed or to whom property rights are granted by means of a trust instrument or some other document.

Grantor: A person who transfers property by deed or grants property rights by means of a trust instrument or some other document.

Guardian: Person appointed to protect the rights (property and person) of a minor.

Holographic Will: A will written by the testator in his own handwriting.

Hypothecation: Generally any pledge to secure an obligation (i.e., hypothecation of securities for a loan).

Indemnity: Protection or exemption from loss or damage.

Interrogatory: A question put in writing.

Inter Vivos Trust: A trust created during the settlor's lifetime—a living trust.

Intestacy: The condition resulting from a person dying without a valid will.

Intestate: Without having left a valid will.

Inurement: Benefiting through the use of.

Irrevocable Trust: A trust which by its terms cannot be revoked by the settlor.

Issue: All persons descending from a common ancestor; broader term than children.

Joint Tenants: Persons who own an equal interest in the same property, all of which passes to the survivor.

Judgment: The decision or sentence of a court of law.

Legacy: A gift of personal property by will, the same as a bequest.

Legal Entity: An association created by law, having a continuous existence independent of the existences of its members and powers and liabilities distinct from those of its members.

Lien: An encumbrance on property.

Liquidation: The process of realizing upon assets and of discharging liabilities in concluding the affairs of a business.

Living Trust: See inter vivos trust.

Margin: The amount paid by a buyer when he uses credit to buy a security.

Notary Public: A public officer who takes acknowledgment of or otherwise attests or certifies deeds and other writings or copies of them; a public officer who takes affidavits and attests signatures of signers.

Nuncupative Will: An oral will by which a person disposes of his property in the event of his death. Some states will not accept nuncupative wills.

Obligee: One to whom an obligation is owed.

Obligor: One who has an obligation to discharge.

Odd Lot: An amount of stock less than the established 100 share unit of trading.

Par Value: The face value of stocks and bonds.

Perpetuity: Duration without limitation as to time.

Personal Property: In the broadest sense, all property other than real property; generally refers to property which is movable.

Portfolio: Total security holdings of an individual or an institution.

Price Earnings Ratio: Current market price of a stock divided by twelve-month earnings per share.

Probate: The judicial procedure to determine that a certain document claimed to be a will of the decedent is, in fact, valid and properly executed; the first step in the settlement of an estate.

Proxy: A person empowered by another to act as his agent in voting shares of stock.

Quitclaim Deed: A form on conveyance of real property whereby the grantor conveys the title only that was vested in the grantor without warranty of title.

Real Property: Any land or estate in land; may be defined to include anything which is immovable (leaseholds, fixtures, and mortgages or other liens on the land).

Remainder Interest: A future interest which will become an interest in possession after the termination of a prior interest created at the same time and by the same instrument as the future interest.

Remainderman: The person designated in a trust agreement to receive the principal at termination of a trust.

Resolution: A formal document expressing the intentions of a board of directors of a corporation.

Reversion: The interest in an estate remaining with the grantor after a particular interest less than the whole estate has been granted by the owner to another person; as distinguished from remainder interest.

Revocable Trust: A trust which may be terminated by the settlor or by another person.

Revocation of a Will: An act by a person who has drawn a will indicating his intention that the will shall no longer be effective.

SEC: Securities and Exchange Commission.

Settlement: The winding down and distribution of an estate by an executor or an administrator.

Settlor: A person who creates a trust (i.e., a living trust operative during a person's lifetime).

Short Term Trust: An irrevocable trust running for a period of at least ten years. The income is payable to a person other than the settlor. Established under the provisions of Revenue Act of 1954.

Spendthrift Clause: Provisions of a will or trust which limit the right of the beneficiary to dispose of his interest, as by assignment, and the right of his creditors to reach it, as by attachment.

Street Name: Stock held in the name of a broker or nominee instead of the legal owner.

Surrogate: The title occasionally given to the judge who presides in the court where estates of deceased persons are administered.

Testamentary Trust: A trust set up by a will; does not become effective until after the death of the will's maker.

Testate: Having left a valid will.

Testator: A person who has left a valid will at his death.

Title: The legal right to ownership of property, real or personal.

Tort: Any wrongful act or omission which causes damage to the person, property, or reputation of another person; private wrong as opposed to public wrong (i.e., crime).

Trust: A fiduciary relationship in which one person (trustee) is the holder of legal title to property (the trust property) subject to an obligation to keep or use the property for the benefit of another person (the beneficiary).

Trustee: The person or corporation who controls or manages a trust for the benefit of specified individuals or organizations.

Trustor: The person who sets up a trust and transfers property to it.

Ultra Vires: Term pertaining to acts of a corporation which exceed its corporate powers.

Vest: To confer an immediate, fixed right to immediate or future possession of property.

Vested Right: To invest or endow a title, function, or power (e.g., the right of a person to own a portion of a contractual pension plan).

Warrant: A paper giving its holder the right to buy a security at a set price, either within a specified period or perpetually. A warrant is generally offered with another security as an added inducement to buy.

Warranty of Title: To guarantee title of an estate or other granted property.

Yield: The return on an investment. To determine the yield on a stock, divide the present indicated annual dividend by the market price of a single share.

APPENDIX

CONTENTS

CORPORATION TAX INFORMATION

SOCIAL SECURITY INFORMATION

INDIVIDUAL TAX INFORMATION

Form **1023** (Rev. May 1977) Department of the Treasury Internal Revenue Service	**Application for Recognition of Exemption** Under Section 501(c)(3) of the Internal Revenue Code	To be filed in the Key District for the area in which the organization has its principal office or place of business.

This application, when properly completed, shall constitute the notice required under section 508(a) of the Internal Revenue Code in order that an applicant may be treated as described in section 501(c)(3) of the Code, and the notice under section 508(b) appropriate to an organization claiming not to be a private foundation within the meaning of section 509(a). **(Read the instructions for each part carefully before making any entries.) The organization must have an organizing instrument (See Part II) before this application may be filed.**

Part I—Identification

1 Full name of organization	2 Employer identification number (If none, attach Form SS-4)
3(a) Address (number and street)	Check here if applying under section: ☐ 501(e) ☐ 501(f)
3(b) City or town, State and ZIP code	4 Name and phone number of person to be contacted

5 Month the annual accounting period ends	6 Date incorporated or formed	7 Activity Codes

8(a) Has the organization filed Federal income tax returns? . . . . ☐ Yes ☐ No

If "Yes," state the form number(s), year(s) filed, and Internal Revenue Office where filed ▶...................................

8(b) Has the organization filed exempt organization information returns? . . . . ☐ Yes ☐ No

If "Yes," state the form number(s), year(s) filed, and Internal Revenue Office where filed ▶...................................

Part II.—Type of Entity and Organizational Documents (See instructions)

Check the applicable entity box below and attach a conformed copy of the organization's organizing and operational documents as indicated for each entity.

☐ Corporation—Articles of incorporation, bylaws. ☐ Trust—Trust indenture. ☐ Other—Constitution or articles, bylaws.

Part III.—Activities and Operational Information

1 What are or will be the organization's sources of financial support? List in order of magnitude. If a portion of the receipts is or will be derived from the earnings of patents, copyrights, or other assets (excluding stock, bonds, etc.), identify such item as a separate source of receipt. Attach representative copies of solicitations for financial support.

2 Describe the organization's fund-raising program, both actual and planned, and explain to what extent it has been put into effect. (Include details of fund-raising activities such as selective mailings, formation of fund-raising committees, use of professional fund raisers, etc.)

I declare under the penalties of perjury that I am authorized to sign this application on behalf of the above organization and I have examined this application, including the accompanying statements, and to the best of my knowledge it is true, correct and complete.

-- (Signature)	-- (Title or authority of signer)	-- (Date)

Part III.—Activities and Operational Information (Continued)

3   Give a narrative description of the activities presently carried on by the organization, and those that will be carried on. If the organization is not fully operational, explain what stage of development its activities have reached, what further steps remain for the organization to become fully operational, and when such further steps will take place. The narrative should specifically identify the services performed or to be performed by the organization. (Do not state the purposes of the organization in general terms or repeat the language of the organizational documents.) If the organization is a school, hospital, or medical research organization, include sufficient information in your description to clearly show that the organization meets the definition of that particular activity that is contained in the instructions for Part VII–A.

---

4   The membership of the organization's governing body is:

(a) Names, addresses, and duties of officers, directors, trustees, etc.	(b) Specialized knowledge, training, expertise, or particular qualifications

Form 1023 (Rev. 5–77)   Page **3**

Part III.—Activities and Operational Information (Continued)

4 **(c)** Do any of the above persons serve as members of the governing body by reason of being public officials or being appointed by public officials? . . . . ☐ Yes ☐ No
If "Yes," please name such persons and explain the basis of their selection or appointment.

(d) Are any members of the organization's governing body "disqualified persons" with respect to the organization (other than by reason of being a member of the governing body) or do any of the members have either a business or family relationship with "disqualified persons"? (See specific instructions 4(d).) . . ☐ Yes ☐ No
If "Yes," please explain.

(e) Have any members of the organization's governing body assigned income or assets to the organization? . ☐ Yes ☐ No
If "Yes," attach a copy of assignment(s) and a list of items assigned.

(f) Is it anticipated that any current or future member of the organization's governing body will assign income or assets to the organization? . . . . ☐ Yes ☐ No
If "Yes," explain fully on an attached sheet.

5 Does the organization control or is it controlled by any other organization? . . . . ☐ Yes ☐ No
Is the organization the outgrowth of another organization, or does it have a special relationship to another organization by reason of interlocking directorates or other factors? . . . . ☐ Yes ☐ No
If either of these questions is answered "Yes," please explain.

6 Is the organization financially accountable to any other organization? . . . . ☐ Yes ☐ No
If "Yes," please explain and identify the other organization. Include details concerning accountability or attach copies of reports if any have been rendered.

7 **(a)** What assets does the organization have that are used in the performance of its exempt function? (Do not include property producing investment income.) If any assets are not fully operational, explain what stage of completion has been reached, what additional steps remain to be completed, and when such final steps will be taken.

(b) To what extent have you used, or do you plan to use contributions as an endowment fund, i.e., hold contributions to produce income for the support of your exempt activities?

8 **(a)** What benefits, services, or products will the organization provide with respect to its exempt function?

Form 1023 (Rev. 5–77)　　　　　　　　　　　　　　　　　　　　　　　　　　　　　　　　　Page 4

Part III.—Activities and Operational Information (Continued)

8 (b) Have the recipients been required or will they be required to pay for the organization's benefits, services, or products? . . . . ☐ Yes ☐ No

If "Yes," please explain and show how the charges are determined.

9 Does or will the organization limit its benefits, services or products to specific classes of individuals? . . . ☐ Yes ☐ No

If "Yes," please explain how the recipients or beneficiaries are or will be selected.

10 Is the organization a membership organization? . . . . ☐ Yes ☐ No

If "Yes," complete the following:

(a) Please describe the organization's membership requirements and attach a schedule of membership fees and dues.

(b) Describe your present and proposed efforts to attract members, and attach a copy of any descriptive literature or promotional material used for this purpose.

(c) Are benefits, services, or products limited to members? . . . . ☐ Yes ☐ No

If "No," please explain.

11 Does or will the organization engage in activities tending to influence legislation or intervene in any way in political campaigns? . . . . ☐ Yes ☐ No

If "Yes," please explain. (Note: *You may wish to file Form 5768, Election/Revocation of Election by an Eligible Section 501(c)(3) Organization to Make Expenditures to Influence Legislation.*)

12 Does the organization have a pension plan for employees? . . . . ☐ Yes ☐ No

13 Are you filing Form 1023 within 15 months from the end of the first month in which you were created or formed as required by section 508(a) and the Regulations thereunder? . . . . ☐ Yes ☐ No

If "No," and you are claiming that section 508(a) does not apply to you, attach an explanation of your basis for this claim.

Part IV.—Statement as to Private Foundation Status

1 Is the organization a private foundation? . . . . ☐ Yes ☐ No

2 If question 1 is answered "No," indicate the type of ruling being requested as to the organization's status under section 509 by checking the applicable box(es) below:

Definite ruling under section 509(a)(1), (2), (3), or (4) check here ☐ and complete Part VII.

Advance ruling under section ▶ ☐ 170(b)(1)(A)(vi) or ▶ ☐ 509(a)(2)—See instructions.

Extended advance ruling under section ▶ ☐ 170(b)(1)(A)(vi) or ▶ ☐ 509(a)(2)—See instructions.

3 If question 1 is answered "Yes," and the organization claims to be a private operating foundation, check here ☐ and complete Part VIII.

(Note: If an extended advance ruling is desired you **must check** the appropriate block for an advance ruling also.)

Form 1023 (Rev. 5-77)   **Part V.—Financial Data**   Page **5**

Statement of Receipts and Expenditures, for period ending ...., 19........

Receipts	1 Gross contributions, gifts, grants and similar amounts received	
	2 Gross dues and assessments of members	
	3 Gross amounts derived from activities related to organization's exempt purpose	
	Less cost of sales	
	4 Gross amounts from unrelated business activities	
	Less cost of sales	
	5 Gross amount received from sale of assets, excluding inventory items (attach schedule) . .	
	Less cost or other basis and sales expenses of assets sold	
	6 Interest, dividends, rents and royalties	
	7 Total receipts	
Expenditures	8 Fund raising expenses	
	9 Contributions, gifts, grants, and similar amounts paid (attach schedule)	
	10 Disbursements to or for benefit of members (attach schedule)	
	11 Compensation of officers, directors, and trustees (attach schedule)	
	12 Other salaries and wages	
	13 Interest	
	14 Rent	
	15 Depreciation and depletion	
	16 Other (attach schedule)	
	17 Total expenditures	
	18 Excess of receipts over expenditures (line 7 less line 17)	

Balance Sheets	Enter dates ▶	Beginning date	Ending date
Assets			
19 Cash (a) Interest bearing accounts			
(b) Other			
20 Accounts receivable, net			
21 Inventories			
22 Bonds and notes (attach schedule)			
23 Corporate stocks (attach schedule)			
24 Mortgage loans (attach schedule)			
25 Other investments (attach schedule)			
26 Depreciable and depletable assets (attach schedule)			
27 Land			
28 Other assets (attach schedule)			
29 Total assets			
Liabilities			
30 Accounts payable			
31 Contributions, gifts, grants, etc., payable			
32 Mortgages and notes payable (attach schedule)			
33 Other liabilities (attach schedules)			
34 Total liabilities			
Fund Balance or Net Worth			
35 Total fund balance or net worth			
36 Total liabilities and fund balance or net worth (line 34 plus line 35) . .			

Has there been any substantial change in any aspect of your financial activities since the period ending date shown above? . . . . ☐ Yes ☐ No
If "Yes," attach a detailed explanation.

Part VI.—Required Schedules for Special Activities	If "Yes," check here;	And, complete schedule—
1 Is the organization, or any part of it, a school?		A
2 Does the organization provide or administer any scholarship benefits, student aid, etc.?		B
3 Has the organization taken over, or will it take over, the facilities of a "for profit" institution? . . .		C
4 Is the organization, or any part of it, a hospital or a medical research organization?		D
5 Is the organization, or any part of it, a home for the aged?		E
6 Is the organization, or any part of it, a litigating organization (public interest law firm or similar organization)? . . .		F
7 Is the organization, or any part of it, formed to promote amateur sports competition?		G

Form 1023 (Rev. 5–77)   Page **6**

Part VII.—Non-Private Foundation Status (Definitive ruling only)

A.—Basis for Non-Private Foundation Status

The organization is not a private foundation because it qualifies as:

	✓	Kind of organization	Within the meaning of	Complete
1		a church	Sections 509(a)(1) and 170(b)(1)(A)(i)	
2		a school	Sections 509(a)(1) and 170(b)(1)(A)(ii)	
3		a hospital	Sections 509(a)(1) and 170(b)(1)(A)(iii)	
4		a medical research organization operated in conjunction with a hospital	Sections 509(a)(1) and 170(b)(1)(A)(iii)	
5		being organized and operated exclusively for testing for public safety	Section 509(a)(4)	
6		being operated for the benefit of a college or university which is owned or operated by a governmental unit	Sections 509(a)(1) and 170(b)(1)(A)(iv)	Part VII.–B
7		normally receiving a substantial part of its support from a governmental unit or from the general public	Sections 509(a)(1) and 170(b)(1)(A)(vi)	Part VII.–B
8		normally receiving not more than one-third of its support from gross investment income and more than one-third of its support from contributions, membership fees, and gross receipts from activities related to its exempt functions (subject to certain exceptions)	Section 509(a)(2)	Part VII.–B
9		being operated solely for the benefit of or in connection with one or more of the organizations described in 1 through 4, or 6, 7, and 8 above	Section 509(a)(3)	Part VII.–C

B.—Analysis of Financial Support

	(a) Most recent taxable year 19........	(Years next preceding most recent taxable year)			(e) Total
		(b) 19........	(c) 19........	(d) 19........	
1 Gifts, grants, and contributions received					
2 Membership fees received					
3 Gross receipts from admissions, sales of merchandise or services, or furnishing of facilities in any activity which is not an unrelated business within the meaning of section 513					
4 Gross income from interest, dividends, rents, royalties, and unrelated business taxable income (less section 511 tax) from businesses acquired by the organization after June 30, 1975					
5 Net income from organization's unrelated business activities not included on line 4					
6 Tax revenues levied for and either paid to or expended on behalf of the organization					
7 Value of services or facilities furnished by a governmental unit to the organization without charge (not including the value of services or facilities generally furnished the public without charge)					
8 Other income (not including gain or loss from sale of capital assets)—attach schedule					
9 Total of lines 1 through 8					
10 Line 9 less line 3					

11 Enter 2% of line 10, column (e) only . . . .

12 If the organization has received any unusual grants during any of the above taxable years, attach a list for each year showing the name of the contributor, the date and amount of grant, and a brief description of the nature of such grant. Do not include such grants in line 1 above. (See instructions)

Form 1023 (Rev. 5–77)   Page **7**

Part VII.—Non-Private Foundation Status (Definitive ruling only) (Continued)

B.—Analysis of Financial Support (Continued)

13 If the organization's non-private foundation status is based upon:

    (a) Sections 509(a)(1) and 170(b)(1)(A)(iv) or (vi).—Attach a list showing the name and amount contributed by each person (other than a governmental unit or "publicly supported" organization) whose total gifts for the entire period exceed the amount shown on line 11.

    (b) Section 509(a)(2).—With respect to the amounts included on lines 1, 2, and 3, attach a list for each of the above years showing the name of and amount received from each person who is a "disqualified person."

    With respect to the amount included in line 3, attach a list for each of the above years showing the name of and amount received from each payor (other than a "disqualified person") whose payments to the organization exceeded $5,000. For this purpose, "payor" includes but is not limited to any organization described in sections 170(b)(1)(A)(i) through (vi) and any government agency or bureau.

C.—Supplemental Information Concerning Organizations Claiming Non-Private Foundation Status Under Section 509(a)(3)

1 Organizations supported by applicant organization: Name and address of supported organization	Has the supported organization received a ruling or determination letter that it is not a private foundation by reason of section 509(a)(1) or (2)?
....	
....	
....	
....	
....	

2 To what extent are the members of your governing board elected or appointed by the supported organization(s)?

3 What is the extent of common supervision or control that you and the supported organization(s) share?

4 To what extent do(es) the supported organization(s) have a significant voice in your investment policies, the making and timing of grants, and in otherwise directing the use of your income or assets?

5 As a result of the supported organization(s) being mentioned in your governing instrument, are you a trust which the supported organization(s) can enforce under State law and with respect to which the supported organization(s) can compel an accounting? . . . . □ **Yes** □ **No**
If "Yes," please explain.

6 What portion of your income do you pay to each supported organization and how significant is such support to each?

7 To what extent do you conduct activities which would otherwise be carried out by the supported organization(s)? For any such activities, please explain your reasoning as to why such activities would otherwise be carried on by the supported organization(s).

8 Is the applicant organization controlled directly or indirectly by one or more "disqualified persons" (other than one who is a disqualified person solely because he or she is a manager) or by an organization which is not described in section 509(a)(1) or (2)? . . . . □ **Yes** □ **No**
If "Yes," please explain.

Form 1023 (Rev. 5–77)   Page **8**

Part VIII.—Basis for Status as a Private Operating Foundation

If the organization—

    (a) bases its claim to private operating foundation status upon normal and regular operations over a period of years; or

    (b) is newly created, set up as a private operating foundation, and has at least one year's experience;

complete the schedule below answering the questions under the income test and one of the three supplemental tests (assets, endowment, or support). If the organization does not have at least one year's experience, complete line 21. If the organization's private operating foundation status depends upon its normal and regular operations as described in (a) above, submit, as an additional attachment, data in tabular form corresponding to the schedule below for the three years next preceding the most recent taxable year.

		Most recent taxable year
Income Test		
1	Adjusted net income, as defined in section 4942(f)	
2	Qualifying distributions:	
	(a) Amounts (including administrative expenses) paid directly for the active conduct of the activities for which organized and operated under section 501(c)(3) (attach schedule)	
	(b) Amounts paid to acquire assets to be used (or held for use) directly in carrying out purposes described in sections 170(c)(1) or 170(c)(2)(B) (attach schedule)	
	(c) Amounts set aside for specific projects which are for purposes described in section 170(c)(1) or 170(c)(2)(B) (attach schedule)	
	(d) Total qualifying distributions (add lines 2(a), (b), and (c))	
3	Percentage of qualifying distributions to adjusted net income (divide line 1 into line 2(d)—percentage must be at least 85 percent)	%
Assets Test		
4	Value of organization's assets used in activities that directly carry out the exempt purposes. Do not include assets held merely for investment or production of income (attach schedule)	
5	Value of any corporate stock of corporation that is controlled by applicant organization and carries out its exempt purposes (attach statement describing such corporation)	
6	Value of all qualifying assets (add lines 4 and 5)	
7	Value of applicant organization's total assets	
8	Percentage of qualifying assets to total assets (divide line 7 into line 6—percentage must exceed 65 percent)	%
Endowment Test		
9	Value of assets not used (or held for use) directly in carrying out exempt purposes:	
	(a) Monthly average of investment securities at fair market value	
	(b) Monthly average of cash balances	
	(c) Fair market value of all other investment property (attach schedule)	
	(d) Total (add lines 9(a), (b), and (c))	
10	Subtract acquisition indebtedness with respect to line 9 items (attach schedule)	
11	Balance (line 9 less line 10)	
12	For years beginning on or after January 1, 1976, multiply line 11 by a factor of 3⅓% (⅔ of the applicable percentage for the minimum investment return computation under section 4942(e)(3)). The factors to be used for years beginning prior to January 1, 1976, are as follows: for 1974 and 1975 use 4%, for 1973 use 3½%. Line 2(d) above must equal or exceed the result of this computation	
Support Test		
13	Applicant organization's support as defined in section 509(d)	
14	Less—amount of gross investment income as defined in section 509(e)	
15	Support for purposes of section 4942(j)(3)(B)(iii)	
16	Support received from the general public, five or more exempt organizations, or a combination thereof (attach schedule)	
17	For persons (other than exempt organizations) contributing more than 1 percent of line 15, enter the total amounts in excess of 1 percent of line 15	
18	Subtract line 17 from line 16	
19	Percentage of total support (divide line 15 into line 18—must be at least 85 percent)	%
20	Does line 16 include support from an exempt organization which is in excess of 25 percent of the amount on line 15?	☐ Yes ☐ No

21 Newly created organizations with less than one year's experience: Attach a statement explaining how the organization is planning to satisfy the requirements of section 4942(j)(3) with respect to the income test and one of the supplemental tests during its first year's operation. Include a description of plans and arrangements, press clippings, public announcements, solicitations for funds, etc.

SCHEDULE A.—Schools, Colleges, and Universities

1 Does or will the organization (or any department or division within it) discriminate in any way on the basis of race with respect to:

    (a) Admissions? . . . . □ Yes □ No

    (b) Use of facilities or exercise of student privileges? . . . . □ Yes □ No

    (c) Faculty or administrative staff? . . . . □ Yes □ No

    (d) Scholarship or loan program? . . . . □ Yes □ No

    If "Yes," for any of the above, please explain.

2 Does the organization include a statement in its charter, bylaws, or other governing instrument, or in a resolution of its governing body, that it has a racially nondiscriminatory policy as to students? . . . . . □ Yes □ No

Attach whatever corporate resolutions or other official statements the organization has made on this subject.

3 **(a)** Has the organization made its racially nondiscriminatory policies known in a manner that brings such policies to the attention of all segments of the general community which it serves? . . . . □ Yes □ No

    If "Yes," please describe how these policies have been publicized and state the frequency with which relevant notices or announcements have been made. If no such newspaper or media notices have been used, please explain.

    (b) If applicable, attach clippings of any relevant newspaper notices or advertising, or copies of tapes or scripts used for media broadcasts. Also attach copies of brochures and catalogues dealing with student admissions, programs, and scholarships, as well as representative copies of all written advertising used as a means of informing prospective students of your programs.

4 Attach a numerical schedule showing the racial composition, as of the current academic year, and projected as far as may be feasible for the subsequent academic year, of: (a) Student body, (b) Faculty and administrative staff.

5 Attach a list showing the amount of scholarship and loan funds, if any, awarded to students enrolled and racial composition of the students who have received such awards.

6 **(a)** Attach a list of the organization's incorporators, founders, board members, and donors of land or buildings, whether individuals or organizations.

    (b) State whether any of the foregoing organizations have as an objective the maintenance of segregated public or private school education, and, if so, whether any of the foregoing individuals are officers or active members of such organizations.

SCHEDULE B.—Organizations Providing Scholarship Benefits, Student Aid, etc. to Individuals

1 **(a)** Please describe the nature of the scholarship benefit, student aid, etc., including the terms and conditions governing its use, whether a gift or a loan, and the amount thereof. If the organization has established or will establish several categories of scholarship benefits, identify each kind of such benefit and explain how the organization determines the recipients for each category. Attach a sample copy of any application the organization requires or will require of individuals to be considered for scholarship grants, loans or similar benefits. (Private foundations which make grants for travel, study or other similar purposes are required to obtain advance approval of scholarship procedures. See sections 53.4945–4 (c) and (d) of the Private Foundation Regulations.)

    (b) If you desire us to consider this application as a request for approval of grant procedures in the event we determine that you are a private foundation, please check here . . . . □

SCHEDULE B.—Organizations Providing Scholarship Benefits, Student Aid, etc. to Individuals (Continued)

2 What limitations or restrictions are there on the class of individuals who are eligible recipients? Specifically explain whether there are, or will be, any restrictions or limitations in the selection procedures based upon race and whether there are, or will be, restrictions or limitations in selection procedures based upon the employment status of the prospective recipient or any relative of the prospective recipient. Also indicate the approximate number of eligible individuals.

3 Indicate the number of grants you anticipate making annually . . . . |

4 List the names, addresses, duties and relevant background of the members of your selection committee. If you base your selections in any way on the employment status of the applicant or any relative of the applicant, indicate whether there is or has been any direct or indirect relationship between the members of the selection committee and the employer. Also indicate whether relatives of the members of the selection committee are possible recipients or have been recipients.

5 Describe any procedures you have for supervising grants, such as obtaining reports or transcripts, which you award and any procedures you have for taking action in the event you discover a failure to live up to the terms of the grant.

SCHEDULE C.—Successors to "For Profit" Institutions

1 What was the name of the predecessor organization and the nature of its activities?

2 Who were the owners or principal stockholders of the predecessor organization? (If more space is needed, attach schedule.)

Name and address	Share or interest

3 Describe the business or family relationship between the owners or principal stockholders and principal employees of the predecessor organization and the officers, directors, and principal employees of the applicant organization.

4 (a) Attach a copy of the agreement of sale or other contract that sets forth the terms and conditions of sale of the predecessor organization or of its assets to the applicant organization.

(b) Attach an appraisal by an independent qualified expert of the facilities or property interest sold showing fair market value at time of sale.

Form 1023 (Rev. 5–77)   Page 11

SCHEDULE C.—Successors to "For Profit" Institutions (Continued)

5 Has any property or equipment formerly used by the predecessor organization been rented to the applicant
organization or will any such property be rented? . . . . □ Yes □ No
   If "Yes," please explain and attach copies of all leases and contracts.

6 Is the organization leasing or will it lease or otherwise make available any space or equipment to the owners, principal stockholders, or principal employees of the predecessor organization? . . . . □ Yes □ No
   If "Yes," please explain and attach a list of such tenants and a copy of the lease for each such tenant.

7 Were any new operating policies initiated as a result of the transfer of assets from a profit-making organization to a nonprofit organization? . . . . □ Yes □ No
   If "Yes," please explain.

SCHEDULE D.—Hospitals and Medical Research Organizations

□ Check here if you are claiming to be a hospital and complete the questions in Part I of this Schedule.
□ Check here if you are claiming to be a medical research organization operated in connection with a hospital and complete the
   questions in Part II of this Schedule.

Part I.—Hospitals

1 (a) How many doctors are on the hospital's courtesy staff? . . . . |_____|
   (b) Do such doctors include all the doctors in the community? . . . . □ Yes □ No
       If "No," please give the reasons why and explain how the courtesy staff is selected.

2 Composition of board of directors or trustees. (If more space is needed, attach schedule.)

Name and address	Occupation

3 (a) Does the hospital maintain a full-time emergency room? . . . . □ Yes □ No
   (b) What is the hospital's policy as to administering emergency services to persons without apparent means
       to pay?

   (c) Does the hospital have any arrangements with police, fire, and voluntary ambulance services as to the de-
       livery or admission of emergency cases? . . . . □ Yes □ No
       Please explain.

Form 1023 (Rev. 5–77)   Page **12**

SCHEDULE D.—Hospitals and Medical Research Organizations (Continued)

Part I.—Hospitals (Continued)

4 **(a)** Does or will the hospital require a deposit from persons covered by Medicare or Medicaid in its admission practices? . . . . ☐ Yes ☐ No

If "Yes," please explain.

(b) Does the same deposit requirement apply to all other patients? . . . . ☐ Yes ☐ No

If "No," please explain.

5 Does or will the hospital provide for a portion of its services and facilities to be used for charity patients? . ☐ Yes ☐ No

Please explain (include data as to the hospital's past experience in admitting charity patients and arrangements it may have with municipal or governmental agencies for absorbing the cost of such care).

6 Does or will the hospital carry on a formal program of medical training and research? . . . . ☐ Yes ☐ No

If "Yes," please describe.

7 Does the hospital provide office space to physicians carrying on a medical practice? . . . . ☐ Yes ☐ No

If "Yes," attach a list setting forth the name of each physician, the amount of space provided, the annual rent (if any), and the expiration of the current lease.

Part II.—Medical Research Organizations

1 Name the hospital(s) with which you have a relationship and describe the relationship(s).

2 Describe your present and proposed (indicate which) medical research activities showing the nature of such activities and the amount of money which has been or will be spent in carrying them out. (Direct conduct of medical research does not include grants to other organizations.)

3 Attach a statement of assets showing the fair market value of your assets and the portion of such assets directly devoted to medical research.

SCHEDULE E.—Homes for Aged

1 What are the requirements for admission to residency? Explain fully and attach promotional literature and application forms.

2 Does or will the home charge an entrance or founder's fee? . . . . · · ☐ Yes ☐ No
If "Yes," please explain.

3 What periodic fees or maintenance charges are or will be required of its residents?

4 (a) What established policy does the home have concerning residents who become unable to pay their regular charges?

   (b) What arrangements does the home have or will it make with local and Federal welfare units, sponsoring organizations, or others to absorb all or part of the cost of maintaining such persons?

5 What arrangements does or will the home have to provide for the health needs of its residents?

6 In what way are the home's residential facilities designed to meet some combination of the physical, emotional, recreational, social, religious, and similar needs of the aged?

7 Has the home established or will it establish any reserves for future expenditures? . . . . ☐ Yes ☐ No
If "Yes," please state the source of such reserves and explain how they will be used.

8 Attach a sample copy of the contract or agreement the organization makes with or requires of its residents.

Form 1023 (Rev. 5–77) Page **14**

SCHEDULE F.—Litigating Organizations (Public Interest Law Firms and Similar Organizations)

1 Will the organization conform to the guidelines for organizations engaged in litigation activities issued by the Internal Revenue Service in Rev. Proc. 71–39, C.B. 1971–2 575, and Rev. Proc. 75–13, 1975–1 C.B. 662? . ☐ Yes ☐ No
If "No," please explain.

2 What is the organization's area of public interest or concern?

3 Is the organization set up primarily to try the case of a particular person or prosecute a particular cause of action? . . . . ☐ Yes ☐ No
If "Yes," please explain.

4 What are the organization's criteria for selection of cases?

5 In what cases has the organization started legal proceedings and in what other cases is it preparing to start proceedings? Please describe the legal issues with respect to each case and explain how they relate to the organization's area of concern.

6 (a) Composition of the organization's board of directors or trustees:

Name and address	Business or Occupation

(b) Will any of the attorneys hired by the organization be a trustee or member of the board of directors of the organization or be associated in the practice of law with any such trustee or member? . . . . . ☐ Yes ☐ No
If "Yes," please explain.

7 Does or will the organization share office space with a private law firm? . . . . ☐ Yes ☐ No
If "Yes," please explain.

8 Does or will the organization receive fees for its professional services? . . . . ☐ Yes ☐ No
If "Yes," please explain.

SCHEDULE G.—National or International Amateur Sports Competition

1 Does your organization provide any facilities or equipment for the use of amateur athletes engaged in national or international sports competition? . . . . ☐ Yes ☐ No
If "Yes," please explain.

Activity Code Numbers of Exempt Organizations (select up to three codes which best describe or most accurately identify your purposes, activities, operations or type of organization and enter in block 7, page 1 of the application. Enter first the code which most accurately identifies you.)

Code

Religious Activities

001 Church, synagogue, etc.
002 Association or convention of churches
003 Religious order
004 Church auxiliary
005 Mission
006 Missionary activities
007 Evangelism
008 Religious publishing activities
 Book store (use 918)
 Genealogical activities (use 094)
029 Other religious activities

Schools, Colleges and Related Activities

030 School, college, trade school, etc
031 Special school for the blind, handicapped, etc.
032 Nursery school
 Day care center (use 574)
033 Faculty group
034 Alumni association or group
035 Parent or parent teachers association
036 Fraternity or sorority
 Key club (use 323)
037 Other student society or group
038 School or college athletic association
039 Scholarships for children of employees
040 Scholarships (other)
041 Student loans
042 Student housing activities
043 Other student aid
044 Student exchange with foreign country
045 Student operated business
 Financial support of schools, colleges, etc (use 602)
 Achievement prizes or awards (use 914)
 Student book store (use 918)
 Student travel (use 299)
 Scientific research (see Scientific Research Activities)
046 Private school
059 Other school related activities

Cultural, Historical or Other Educational Activities

060 Museum, zoo, planetarium, etc
061 Library
062 Historical site, records or reenactment
063 Monument
064 Commemorative event (centennial, festival, pageant, etc)
065 Fair
088 Community theatrical group
089 Singing society or group
090 Cultural performances
091 Art exhibit
092 Literary activities
093 Cultural exchanges with foreign country
094 Genealogical activities
 Achievement prizes or awards (use 914)
 Gifts or grants to individuals (use 561)
 Financial support of cultural organizations (use 602)
119 Other cultural or historical activities

Other Instruction and Training Activities

120 Publishing activities
121 Radio or television broadcasting
122 Producing films
123 Discussion groups, forums, panels, lectures, etc
124 Study and research (non scientific)
125 Giving information or opinion (see also Advocacy)
126 Apprentice training
 Travel tours (use 299)
149 Other instruction and training

Health Services and Related Activities

150 Hospital
151 Hospital auxiliary
152 Nursing or convalescent home
153 Care and housing for the aged (see also 382)
154 Health clinic
155 Rural medical facility
156 Blood bank
157 Cooperative hospital service organization
158 Rescue and emergency service
159 Nurses' register or bureau
160 Aid to the handicapped (see also 031)
161 Scientific research (diseases)
162 Other medical research
163 Health insurance (medical, dental, optical, etc)
164 Prepaid group health plan
165 Community health planning
166 Mental health care
167 Group medical practice association
168 In faculty group practice association
169 Hospital pharmacy, parking facility, food services, etc.
179 Other health services

Code

Scientific Research Activities

180 Contract or sponsored scientific research for industry
181 Scientific research for government
 Scientific research (diseases) (use 161)
199 Other scientific research activities

Business and Professional Organizations

200 Business promotion (chamber of commerce, business league, etc)
201 Real estate association
202 Board of trade
203 Regulating business
204 Better Business Bureau
205 Professional association
206 Professional association auxiliary
207 Industry trade shows
208 Convention displays
 Testing products for public safety (use 905)
209 Research, development and testing
210 Professional athletic league
 Attracting new industry (use 403)
 Publishing activities (use 120)
 Insurance or other benefits for members (see Employee or Membership Benefit Organizations)
211 Underwriting municipal insurance
212 Assigned risk insurance activities
213 Tourist bureau
229 Other business or professional group

Farming and Related Activities

230 Farming
231 Farm bureau
232 Agricultural group
233 Horticultural group
234 Farmers' cooperative marketing or purchasing
235 Financing crop operations
 FFA, FHA, 4–H club, etc. (use 322)
 Fair (use 065)
236 Dairy herd improvement association
237 Breeders association
249 Other farming and related activities

Mutual Organizations

250 Mutual ditch, irrigation, telephone, electric company or like organization
251 Credit Union
252 Reserve funds or insurance for domestic building and loan association, cooperative bank, or mutual savings bank
253 Mutual insurance company
254 Corporation organized under an Act of Congress (see also 904)
 Farmers' cooperative marketing or purchasing (use 234)
 Cooperative hospital service organization (use 157)
259 Other mutual organization

Employee or Membership Benefit Organizations

260 Fraternal beneficiary society, order, or association
261 Improvement of conditions of workers
262 Association of municipal employees
263 Association of employees
264 Employee or member welfare association
265 Sick, accident, death, or similar benefits
266 Strike benefits
267 Unemployment benefits
268 Pension or retirement benefits
269 Vacation benefits
279 Other services or benefits to members or employees

Sports, Athletic, Recreational and Social Activities

280 Country club
281 Hobby club
282 Dinner club
283 Variety club
284 Dog club
285 Women's club
 Garden club (use 356)
286 Hunting or fishing club
287 Swimming or tennis club
288 Other sports club
 Boys Club, Little League, etc (use 321)
296 Community center
297 Community recreational facilities (park, playground, etc)
298 Training in sports
299 Travel tours
300 Amateur athletic association
 School or college athletic association (use 038)
301 Fund raising athletic or sports event
317 Other sports or athletic activities
318 Other recreational activities
319 Other social activities

Code

Youth Activities

320 Boy Scouts, Girl Scouts, etc
321 Boys Club, Little League, etc
322 FFA, FHA, 4–H club, etc
323 Key club
324 YMCA, YWCA, YMHA, etc
325 Camp
326 Care and housing of children (orphanage, etc)
327 Prevention of cruelty to children
328 Combat juvenile delinquency
349 Other youth organization or activities

Conservation, Environmental and Beautification Activities

350 Preservation of natural resources (conservation)
351 Combatting or preventing pollution (air, water, etc)
352 Land acquisition for preservation
353 Soil or water conservation
354 Preservation of scenic beauty
 Litigation (see Litigation and Legal Aid Activities)
 Combat community deterioration (use 402)
355 Wildlife sanctuary or refuge
356 Garden club
379 Other conservation, environmental or beautification activities

Housing Activities

380 Low income housing
381 Low and moderate income housing
382 Housing for the aged (see also 153)
 Nursing or convalescent home (use 152)
 Student housing (use 042)
 Orphanage (use 326)
398 Instruction and guidance on housing
399 Other housing activities

Inner City or Community Activities

400 Area development, re-development or renewal
 Housing (see Housing Activities)
401 Homeowners association
402 Other activity aimed at combatting community deterioration
403 Attracting new industry or retaining industry in an area
404 Community promotion
 Community recreational facility (use 297)
 Community center (use 296)
405 Loans or grants for minority businesses
 Job training, counseling, or assistance (use 566)
 Day care center (use 574)
 Civil rights activity (see Civil Rights Activities)
 Referral service (social agencies) (use 569)
 Legal aid to indigents (use 462)
406 Crime prevention
407 Volunteer firemen's organization or auxiliary
 Rescue squad (use 158)
408 Community service organization
429 Other inner city or community benefit activities

Civil Rights Activities

430 Defense of human and civil rights
431 Elimination of prejudice and discrimination, race, religion, sex, national origin, etc.)
432 Lessen neighborhood tensions
 Litigation (see Litigation and Legal Aid Activities)
 Legislative and political activities (see that caption)
449 Other civil rights activities

Litigation and Legal Aid Activities

460 Public interest litigation activities
461 Other litigation or support of litigation
462 Legal aid to indigents
463 Providing bail

Legislative and Political Activities

480 Propose, support, or oppose legislation
481 Voter information on issues or candidates
482 Voter education (mechanics of registering, voting, etc.)
483 Support, oppose, or rate political candidates
484 Provide facilities or services for political campaign activities
509 Other legislative and political activities

Advocacy

Attempt to influence public opinion concerning:

Code

510 Firearms control
511 Selective Service System
512 National defense policy
513 Weapons systems
514 Government spending
515 Taxes or tax exemption
516 Separation of church and state
517 Government aid to parochial schools
518 U S foreign policy
519 U S military involvement
520 Pacifism and peace
521 Economic political system of U S
522 Anti communism
523 Right to work
524 Zoning or rezoning
525 Location of highway or transportation system
526 Rights of criminal defendants
527 Capital punishment
528 Stricter law enforcement
529 Ecology or conservation
530 Protection of consumer interests
531 Medical care system
532 Welfare system
533 Urban renewal
534 Busing students to achieve racial balance
535 Racial integration
536 Use of intoxicating beverage
537 Use of drugs or narcotics
538 Use of tobacco
539 Prohibition of erotica
540 Sex education in public schools
541 Population control
542 Birth control methods
543 Legalized abortion
559 Other matters

Other Activities Directed to Individuals

560 Supplying money, goods or services to the poor
561 Gifts or grants to individuals (other than scholarships)
 Scholarships for children of employees (use 039)
 Scholarships (other) (use 040)
 Student loans (use 041)
562 Other loans to individuals
563 Marriage counseling
564 Family planning
565 Credit counseling and assistance
566 Job training, counseling, or assistance
567 Draft counseling
568 Vocational counseling
569 Referral service (social agencies)
572 Rehabilitating convicts or ex convicts
573 Rehabilitating alcoholics, drug abusers, compulsive gamblers, etc.
574 Day care center
575 Services for the aged (see also 153 and 382)
 Training of or aid to the handicapped (see 031 and 160)

Activities Directed to Other Organizations

600 Community Chest, United Givers Fund, etc.
601 Booster club
602 Gifts, grants, or loans to other organizations
603 Non-financial services or facilities to other organizations

Other Purposes and Activities

900 Cemetery or burial activities
901 Perpetual care fund (cemetery, columbarium, etc.)
902 Emergency or disaster aid fund
903 Community trust or component
904 Government instrumentality or agency (see also 254)
905 Testing products for public safety
906 Consumer interest group
907 Veterans activities
908 Patriotic activities
909 Non exempt trust
910 Domestic organization with activities outside U.S.
911 Foreign organization
912 Title holding corporation
913 Prevention of cruelty to animals
914 Achievement prizes or awards
915 Erection or maintenance of public building or works
916 Cafeteria, restaurant, snack bar, food services, etc.
917 Thrift shop, retail outlet, etc.
918 Book, gift or supply store
919 Advertising
920 Association of employees
921 Loans or credit reporting
922 Endowment fund or financial services
923 Indians (tribes, cultures, etc.)
924 Traffic or tariff bureau

U S GOVERNMENT PRINTING OFFICE 1977-O-575-270-87-0321919

90 of the Treasury enue Service	**Return of Organization Exempt from Income Tax** Under section 501(c) (except black lung benefit trust or private foundation), 501(e) or (f) of the Internal Revenue Code	**1980**

alendar year 1980, or fiscal year beginning _____ , 1980, and ending _____ , 19 ___

Name of organization	**A** Employer identification number (see instructions)
Address (number and street)	**B** If exemption application is pending, check here. . . . . ▶
City or town, State, and ZIP code	**C** If address changed check here. . . ▶

applicable box—Exempt under section ▶ ☐ 501(c) ( ) (insert number), ☐ 501(e) **OR** ☐ 501(f).

a group return (see instruction I) filed for affiliates? . . ☐ Yes ☐ No   If "Yes" to either, give four-digit group exemption
a separate return filed by a group affiliate? . . . . . ☐ Yes ☐ No   number (GEN) ▶

here if gross receipts are normally not more than $10,000 and do not complete the rest of this return (see instruction B(11)).
here if gross receipts are normally more than $10,000 and line 12 is $25,000 or less. Complete Parts I, II, IV, and VI and only the indicated items in Parts III
(see instruction H). If line 12 is more than $25,000, complete the entire return.

501(c)(3) organizations must also complete Schedule A (Form 990) and attach it to this return.

Analysis of Revenue, Expenses, and Fund Balances			(A) Total	(B) Restricted/ Nonexpendable	(C) Unrestricted/ Expendable
Contributions, gifts, grants, and similar amounts received:					
(a) Directly from the public					
(b) Through professional fundraisers					
(c) As allotments from fundraising organizations .					
(d) As government grants					
(e) Other					
(f) Total (add lines 1(a) through 1(e)) (attach schedule—see instructions) .					
Membership dues and assessments					
Interest					
Dividends					
(a) Gross rents					
(b) Minus: Rental expenses					
(c) Net rental income (loss)					
Royalties					
(a) Gross amount received from sale of assets other than inventory					
(b) Minus: Cost or other basis and sales expenses .					
(c) Net gain (loss) (attach schedule)					
Special fundraising events and activities (itemize):					

Type of event	Receipts	Expenses

(a) Total receipts					
(b) Total expenses					
(c) Net income (line 8(a) minus line 8(b))					
(a) Gross sales minus returns and allowances . .					
(b) Minus: Cost of goods sold (attach schedule) .					
(c) Gross profit (loss)					
Program service revenue (from Part II, line (f))					
Other revenue (from Part II, line (g))					
Total revenue (add lines 1(f), 2, 3, 4, 5(c), 6, 7(c), 8(c), 9(c), 10, and 11) . .					
Fundraising (from line 40(B))					
Program services (from line 40(C))					
Management and general (from line 40(D))					
Total expenses (from line 40(A))					
Excess (deficit) for the year (subtract line 16 from line 12) . . .					
Fund balances or net worth at beginning of year (from line 65(A)) .					
Other changes in fund balances or net worth (attach explanation) . .					
Fund balances or net worth at end of year (add lines 17, 18, and 19) .					

Form 990 (1980)

Part II Program Service Revenue and Other Revenue (State Nature)	Program service revenue	Other re
(a)		
(b)		
(c)		
(d)		
(e)		
(f) Total program service revenue (Enter here and on line 10)		
(g) Total other revenue (Enter here and on line 11)		

Part III Allocation of Expenses by Function

If line 12, Part I is $25,000 or less, you should complete only the line item umns (A) and (B), Part III. If line 12 is more than $25,000, complete columns (C), and (D).

Do not include amounts reported on line 5(b), 7(b), 8(b), or 9(b) of Part I.	(A) Total	(B) Fundraising	(C) Program services	(D) Mana and ge
21 Contributions, gifts, grants, and similar amounts awarded (attach schedule) . . .				
22 Benefits paid to or for members				
23 Compensation of officers, directors, and trustees				
24 Other salaries and wages				
25 Pension plan contributions				
26 Other employee benefits				
27 Payroll taxes				
28 Fees for fundraising				
29 Other professional services				
30 Interest				
31 Occupancy				
32 Rental and maintenance of equipment . . .				
33 Printing and postage				
34 Telephone				
35 Supplies				
36 Travel				
37 Other expenses (itemize):				
....				
....				
....				
....				
38 Total expenses before depreciation (add lines 21 through 37)				
39 Depreciation, depletion, etc.				
40 Total (add lines 38 and 39). Enter here and on lines 13 through 16				

(Expenses)

Part IV List of Officers, Directors, and Trustees (See Instructions)

(A) Name and address	(B) Title and time spent on position	(C) Compensation	(D) Contributions to employee benefit plans	(E) Expense and ot allowar
....				
....				
....				
....				
....				
....				

90 (1980)   Page **3**

| **V** | **Balance Sheet** | If line 12, Part I is $25,000 or less, you should complete only lines 53 and 60 and, if you do not use fund accounting, line 64. If line 12 is more than $25,000, complete the entire balance sheet. |

Assets	(A) Beginning of tax year	(B) End of tax year
sh:		
Savings and interest-bearing accounts		
Other		
counts receivable:		
Beginning receivables ▶..................... minus allowance for doubtful accounts ▶....................		
Ending receivables ▶..................... minus allowance for doubtful accounts ▶....................		
tes receivable:		
Beginning receivables ▶..................... minus allowance for doubtful accounts ▶....................		
Ending receivables ▶..................... minus allowance for doubtful accounts ▶....................		
Loans to officers, directors, and trustees (attach schedule)................		
entories		
vernment obligations:		
U.S. and instrumentalities		
State and its subdivisions		
estments in corporate bonds, etc. (attach schedule)		
vestments in corporate stocks (attach schedule)		
ortgage loans (number of loans ▶.................)		
her investments (attach schedule)		
preciable (depletable) assets (attach schedule):		
Beginning assets ▶..................... minus accumulated depreciation ▶....................		
Ending assets ▶..................... minus accumulated depreciation ▶....................		
nd		
her assets (attach schedule)		
tal assets		
Liabilities		
counts payable		
ntributions, gifts, grants, etc., payable		
nds and notes payable (attach schedule)		
ortgages payable		
ans from officers, directors, and trustees (attach schedule)		
her liabilities (attach schedule)		
tal liabilities		

Fund Balances and Net Worth		
ete this section of the balance sheet based on the accounting method you normally use. check either "Fund Accounting" or "All Others," and give the information requested under x you checked.		

Fund Accounting	All Others		
here . . . . ▶ ☐	Check here . . . . ▶ ☐		
rrent funds:			
) Unrestricted			
) Restricted			
nd, buildings, and equipment	Capital stock or trust principal		
dowment and similar funds	Paid-in or capital surplus		
her	Retained earnings or accumulated income		
tal fund balances	Total net worth		
tal liabilities and fund balances or net worth		

Form 990 (1980)

Part VI Statements About Activities		Ye

67 Describe each significant program service activity and indicate the total expenses paid or incurred in connection with each: | Expenses |
- (a) .... | ....
- (b) .... | ....
- (c) .... | ....
- (d) .... | ....

68 Has the organization engaged in any activities not previously reported to the Internal Revenue Service? . . . .
If "Yes," attach a detailed description of the activities.

69 Have any changes been made in the organizing or governing documents, but not reported to IRS? . . . .
If "Yes," attach a conformed copy of the changes.

70 (a) Did the organization have unrelated business gross income of $1,000 or more during the year covered by this return? .
  (b) If "Yes," have you filed a tax return on Form 990–T, Exempt Organization Business Income Tax Return, for this year? .
  (c) If the organization has gross sales or receipts from business activities not reported on Form 990–T, attach a statement explaining your reason for not reporting them on Form 990–T.

71 Was there a liquidation, dissolution, termination, or substantial contraction during the year (see instructions)? . . . .
If "Yes," attach a statement as described in the instructions.

72 Is the organization related (other than by association with a statewide or nationwide organization) through common membership, governing bodies, trustees, officers, etc., to any other exempt or nonexempt organization (see instructions)? . . .
If "Yes," enter the name of organization ▶..
.... and check whether it is ☐ exempt OR ☐ nonexempt.

73 (a) Enter any political expenditures, direct or indirect, as described in the instructions . . . . |
  (b) Did you file Form 1120–POL, U.S. Income Tax Return of Certain Political Organizations, for this year? .

74 Did your organization receive donated services or the use of facilities or equipment at no charge or at substantially less than fair rental value? . . . .
If "Yes," you may, if you choose, indicate the value of these items here. Do not include this amount elsewhere on this return . . . . ▶

The following statements should be completed ONLY for the organizations indicated.

75 Section 501(c)(5) or (6) organizations.—Did the organization spend any amounts in an attempt to influence public opinion about legislative matters or referendums (see instructions and Regulations section 1.162–20(c))? . . . .
If "Yes," enter the total amount spent for this purpose . . . . |

76 Section 501(c)(7) organizations.—Enter amount of:
  (a) Initiation fees and capital contributions included on line 12 . |
  (b) Gross receipts, included in line 12, for public use of club facilities (see instructions) . . . . . |
  (c) Does the club's governing instrument or any written policy statement provide for discrimination against any person because of race, color, or religion? . . . .

77 Section 501(c)(12) organizations.—Enter amount of:
  (a) Gross income received from members or shareholders . . . . |
  (b) Gross income received from other sources (do not net amounts due or paid to other sources against amounts due or received from them) . . . . |

78 Public interest law firms.—Attach information described in instructions.

79 The books are in care of ▶................................. Telephone No. ▶.................................
Located at ▶

Please Sign Here	Under penalties of perjury, I declare that I have examined this return, including accompanying schedules and statements, and to the best of my knowledge it is true, correct, and complete. Declaration of preparer (other than taxpayer) is based on all information of which preparer has any knowledge.		
	Signature of officer	Date ▶ Title	
Paid Preparer's Use Only	Preparer's signature and date ▶		
	Firm's name (or yours, if self-employed) and address ▶	Check if self-employed ▶ ☐	
		ZIP code ▶	

✿U.S. GOVERNMENT PRINTING OFFICE: 1980–313–050 E.I. 43-0797287

90-T
of the Treasury
enue Service

Exempt Organization Business Income Tax Return (Under Section 511 of the Internal Revenue Code)

For calendar year 1980 or fiscal year beginning.................................
1980, and ending .... , 19 ......

1980

organization

	A Employer identification number (employees' trust see instruction for Block A)
number and street)	
wn, State, and ZIP code	**B** Enter unrelated business activity codes from page 8 of instructions

box if address changed . . . . ▶ ☐   **D** Exempt under section . . . . . . ▶ 501 ( )( )

applicable box . . . . ▶ ☐ Corporation ☐ Trust   **F** Group exemption number (see instructions for Block F) ▶

Complete page 1, Schedule K on page 2, and sign the return if the unrelated trade or business gross income is $10,000 or less.
Complete all applicable parts of the form (except lines 1 through 5) if unrelated trade or business gross income is over $10,000.

ed Business Taxable Income Computation—When Unrelated Trade or Business Gross Income is $10,000 or Less

ated trade or business gross income. (State sources ....)	1	
deductions	2	
ated business taxable income before specific deduction	3	
specific deduction (see instructions for line 32)	4	
ated business taxable income	5	

Organizations Taxable as Corporations (See Instructions for Tax Computation)

(a) Are you a member of a controlled group? . . . . ☐ Yes . . . . . ☐ No

(b) If "Yes," see instructions and enter your share of the $25,000 amount in each taxable income bracket:
(i) $.......................... (ii) $........................... (iii) $........................... (iv) $...........................

Income tax on amount on line 5 above, or line 33, page 2, whichever applies. Check here ▶ ☐ if alternative tax from Schedule D (Form 1120) is used	7	

Trusts Taxable at Trust Rates (See Instructions for Tax Computation) Section 401(a) trust, check here ▶ ☐

Enter the tax from the tax rate schedule in instructions on amount on line 5 above, or line 33 on page 2, whichever applies .	8	

(a) Foreign tax credit (corporations attach Form 1118, trusts attach Form 1116)	9(a)		
(b) Investment credit (attach Form 3468)	9(b)		
(c) Work incentive (WIN) credit (attach Form 4874)	9(c)		
(d) Other credits (see instructions)	9(d)		
Total (add lines 9(a) through (d))		10	
Subtract line 10 from line 7 or line 8		11	
Increase in tax from refiguring an earlier year investment credit (attach Form 4255)		12	
Minimum tax on tax preference items (see instructions for line 13) . . . . , .		13	
Alternative minimum tax (see instructions for line 14)		14	
Total tax (add lines 11 through 14)		15	
Credits and payments: (a) Tax deposited with Form 7004	16(a)		
(b) Tax deposited with Form 7005 (attach copy)	16(b)		
(c) Foreign organizations—Tax paid or withheld at the source (see instructions) .	16(c)		
(d) Credit from regulated investment companies (attach Form 2439)	16(d)		
(e) Federal tax on special fuels and oils (attach Form 4136)	16(e)		
(f) Other payments and credits (see instructions)	16(f)		
(g) Total credits and payments (add lines 16(a) through 16(f))		16(g)	
TAX DUE (Subtract line 16(g) from line 15. See instructions for depositary method of payment ▶		17	
If line 16(g) is more than line 15, enter OVERPAYMENT . . . . ▶		18	

ents Regarding Certain Activities

	Yes	No
ay time during the tax year, did you have an interest in or a signature or other authority over a bank account, securities nt, or other financial account in a foreign country (see instructions)?		
ou the grantor of or transferor to a foreign trust which existed during the current tax year, whether or not you have any beneficial interest in it? . es," you may have to file Forms 3520, 3520–A or 926.		

Under penalties of perjury, I declare that I have examined this return, including accompanying schedules and statements, and to the best of my knowledge and belief, it is true, correct, and complete. Declaration of preparer (other than taxpayer) is based on all information of which preparer has any knowledge.

▶ Signature of officer	Date ▶ Title	
Preparer's signature and date ▶	Check if self-employed ▶ ☐	Preparer's social security no.
Firm's name (or yours, if self-employed) and address ▶	E.I. No. ▶	
	ZIP code ▶	

Form 990–T (1980)　　　　　　　　　　　　　　　　　　　　　　　　　　　　　　　　　　　Pag

Unrelated Business Taxable Income Computation

Unrelated Trade or Business Income

1 Gross receipts or gross sales ...., minus returns and allowances........................ Balance ▶	1	
2 Minus: Cost of goods sold (Schedule A) and operations (attach schedule)	2	
3 Gross profit	3	
4 (a) Capital gain net income (attach separate Schedule D)	4(a)	
(b) Net gain or (loss) from Part II, Form 4797 (attached)	4(b)	
(c) Capital loss deduction for trusts	4(c)	
5 Income or (loss) from partnerships (attach statement)	5	
6 Rent income (Schedule C)	6	
7 Unrelated debt-financed income (Schedule E, line 2)	7	
8 Investment income of a section 501(c)(7) or (9) organization (Schedule F)	8	
9 Interest, annuities, royalties, and rents from controlled organizations (Schedule G)	9	
10 Exploited exempt activity income (Schedule H)	10	
11 Advertising income (Schedule I, Part III, Column A)	11	
12 Other income (see instructions for line 12—attach schedule)	12	
13　　　TOTAL unrelated trade or business income (add lines 3 through 12)	13	

Deductions Not Taken Elsewhere

(Except for contributions, deductions must be directly connected with the unrelated business income)

14 Compensation of officers, directors and trustees (Schedule J)	14	
15 Salaries and wages ...., minus WIN credit .... Balance ▶	15	
16 Repairs (see instructions)	16	
17 Bad debts (see instructions)	17	
18 Interest (attach schedule)	18	
19 Taxes	19	
20 Contributions (see instructions for line 20)	20	
21 Depreciation (attach Form 4562)	21	
22 Amortization (attach schedule)	22	
23 Depletion	23	
24 (a) Contributions to deferred compensation plans (see instructions for line 24(a))	24(a)	
(b) Employee benefit programs (see instructions for line 24(b))	24(b)	
25 Other deductions (attach schedule)	25	
26　　　TOTAL deductions (add lines 14 through 25)	26	
27 Unrelated business taxable income before allowable advertising loss (subtract line 26 from line 13) . .	27	
28 Minus: Advertising loss (Schedule I, Part III, Column B)	28	
29 Unrelated business taxable income before net operating loss deduction (subtract line 28 from line 27) . .	29	
30 Minus: Net operating loss deduction (see instructions for line 30)	30	
31 Unrelated business taxable income before specific deduction (subtract line 30 from line 29)	31	
32 Minus: Specific deduction (see instructions for line 32)	32	
33 Unrelated business taxable income (subtract line 32 from line 31)	33	

Schedule A—COST OF GOODS SOLD (See Instructions for Line 2 above)

Schedule K—RECORD OF FEDERAL TAX DEPOSIT FORMS 503
(List deposits in order of date made—See Instruction for line 17, pa

Method of inventory valuation (specify) ▶

		Date of deposit	Amount
1 Inventory at beginning of year			
2 Merchandise bought for manufacture or sale . . .			
3 Salaries and wages			
4 Other costs (attach schedule)			
5　　TOTAL			
6 Minus inventory at end of year			
7 Cost of goods sold (enter here and on line 2, above) .			

The books are in care of ▶　　　　　　　　　　　　　　Telephone number ▶

)–T (1980)   Page **3**

ule C—RENT INCOME FROM REAL PROPERTY AND PERSONAL PROPERTY LEASED WITH REAL PROPERTY
(See Instructions for line 6 of page 2)

1. Description of property	2. Rent received or accrued	3. Percentage of rent for personal property
		%
		%
		%
		%
		%

Complete for any item if the entry in column 3 is more than 50%, or if the rent is based on profit or income		5. Complete for any item if the entry in column 3 is more than 10% but not more than 50%		
uctions directly con- (Attach schedule)	(b) Income includible (Column 2 minus column 4(a))	(a) Gross income reportable (Column 2 × column 3)	(b) Deductions directly connected with personal property (Attach schedule)	(c) Income includible (Column 5(a) minus column 5(b))

d columns 4(b) and 5(c) and enter total here and on line 6, page 2 . . . .

ule E—UNRELATED DEBT-FINANCED INCOME. (See Instructions for line 7 of page 2)

1. Description of debt financed property	2. Gross income from or allocable to debt-financed property	3. Deductions directly connected with or allocable to debt financed property	
		(a) Straight line depreciation (Attach schedule)	(b) Other deductions (Attach schedule)

4. Amount of average acquisition indebtedness on or allocable to debt financed property (Attach schedule)	5. Average adjusted basis of or allocable to debt financed property (Attach schedule)	6. Percentage which column 4 is of column 5	7. Gross income reportable (Column 2 × column 6)	8. Allocable deductions (Total of columns 3(a) and 3(b) × column 6)	9. Net income or (loss) includible (Column 7 minus column 8)
		%			
		%			
		%			
		%			

tal (enter here and on line 7, page 2) . . . .
tal dividends-received deductions included in column 8 . . . .

ule F—INVESTMENT INCOME OF A SECTION 501(c)(7) OR (9) ORGANIZATION (See Instructions for Line 8 of Page 2)

(a) Description	(b) Amount	(c) Deductions directly connected (Attach schedule)	(d) Net investment income (Column (b) minus column (c))	(e) Set asides (Attach schedule)	(f) Balance of investment income (Column (d) minus column (e))

tal (enter here and on line 8, page 2) . . . .

ule G—INCOME (ANNUITIES, INTEREST, RENTS AND ROYALTIES) FROM CONTROLLED ORGANIZATIONS
(See Instructions for Line 9 of Page 2)

1. Name and address of controlled organization(s)	2. Gross income from controlled organization(s)	3. Deductions of controlling organization directly connected with column 2 income (Attach schedule)	4. Exempt controlled organizations		
			(a) Unrelated business taxable income	(b) Taxable income computed as though not exempt under section 501(a) or the amount in column (a), whichever is more	(c) Percentage which column (a) is of column (b)
					%
					%
					%

5. Nonexempt controlled organizations			6. Gross income reportable (Column 2 × column 4(c) or column 5(c))	7. Allowable deductions (Column 3 × column 4(c) or column 5(c))	8. Net income includible (Column 6 minus column 7)
(a) Excess taxable income	(b) Taxable income or amount in column (a), whichever is more	(c) Percent age which column (a) is of column (b)			
		%			
		%			
		%			

tal (enter here and on line 9, page 2) . . . .

Form 990-T (1980)

Schedule H—EXPLOITED EXEMPT ACTIVITY INCOME, OTHER THAN ADVERTISING INCOME
(See Instructions for Line 10 of Page 2)

1. Description of exploited activity	2. Gross un-related business income from trade or business	3. Expenses di-rectly connected with production of unrelated business income	4. Net income from unrelated trade or business (Column 2 minus column 3)	5. Gross income from activity that is not unrelated business income	6. Expenses at-tributable to column 5	7. Excess exempt expenses (Column 6 minus column 5 but not more than column 4)	8. Net includible 4 minus

Total (enter here and on line 10, page 2) . . . .

Schedule I—ADVERTISING INCOME AND ADVERTISING LOSS (See Instructions for Line 11 of Page 2)
Part I—Income from periodicals reported on consolidated basis

1. Name of periodical	2. Gross adver-tising income	3. Direct adver-tising costs	4. Advertising gain or loss (col. 2 minus col. 3). If loss, enter in col. B, Part III. Do not complete cols. 5, 6 and 7. If gain, complete cols. 5, 6 and 7.	5. Circulation income	6. Reader-ship costs	7. If col. 5 col. 6, enter A, Part III, shown in col. 6 exceeds co-tract col. 6 pl from col. 5 2. Enter gain Part III

Totals . . . . .

Part II—Income from periodicals reported on a separate basis

Part III—Column A—Advertising Income		Part III—Column B—Advertising Loss	
(a) Enter "consolidated periodical" or names of non-consolidated periodicals	(b) Enter total amount from col-umn 4 or 7, Part I and amounts listed in cols. 4 and 7, Part II	(a) Enter "consolidated periodical" or names of non-consolidated periodicals	(b) Enter total amount from 4, Part I and amounts liste umn 4, Part II
Enter total here and on line 11, page 2		Enter total here and on line 28, page 2	

Schedule J—COMPENSATION OF OFFICERS, DIRECTORS AND TRUSTEES

1. Name	2. Title	3. Time devoted to business	4. Total comp

Total compensation of officers (enter total here and on line 14, page 2) . . . .

Department of the Treasury
Internal Revenue Service

Publication 517
Rev. Nov. 80)

Social Security for Members of the Clergy and Religious Workers

For use in preparing
1980 Returns

You can get the tax forms and publications referred to in this publication by writing to the IRS Forms Distribution Center listed in your Form 1040 or 1040A Instructions. Or, you can call the Tax Information number in the phone book listed under "United States Government, Internal Revenue Service."

Introduction

This publication discusses social security coverage and self-employment tax for the clergy.

It also tells you how, as a member of the clergy (minister, member of a religious order, or Christian Science practitioner), to apply for an exemption from social security coverage if you did not elect coverage previously for years before 1968.

A discussion of net earnings from self-employment and of tax returns also is included.

Social Security Coverage

Social security tax is collected under two separate tax systems. Under the Federal Insurance Contributions Act (FICA), half the tax is paid by the employee and the other half is paid by the employer. Under the Self-Employment Contributions Act, the total tax is paid by the self-employed person.

The earnings that you receive for performing services in the exercise of the ministry are subject to self-employment tax unless you are a member of a religious order who has taken a vow of poverty, or unless you request and receive from the Internal Revenue Service an exemption from self-employment tax. See *Exemption from Social Security Coverage*, later in this publication.

Although members of the clergy are treated as self-employed individuals or persons in the performance of their ministerial services for social security purposes, they may be treated as employees for other tax purposes. For example, a minister who is hired and paid by a church to perform services for it, subject to its right of control, is an employee of the church in the performance of those services. Form W-2 is the correct form to use to report the wages paid by the church to its employee, the minister. However, the minister is treated as self-employed for social security purposes and pays self-employment tax on the wages paid by the church.

It is possible for ministers who are employees of their churches to be self-employed in their performance of services outside their activities as employees. For example, a minister may receive amounts directly from members of the church (such as fees for performing marriages, baptisms, or other personal services) that are earnings from self-employment for all tax purposes.

Ministers

As a duly ordained, commissioned, or licensed minister of a church you are covered by social security under the self-employment provisions for the services you perform in your capacity as a minister. For the specific services covered, see *Services to Which Coverage or Exemption Applies*, discussed later.

A minister of the gospel is an individual who is duly ordained, commissioned, or licensed to the pastoral ministry by action of a religious body constituting a church or church denomination and invested with authority to conduct religious worship, to perform sacerdotal functions, and to administer ordinances or sacraments according to the prescribed tenets and principles of that church or church denomination.

If a church or church denomination ordains some ministers of the gospel and licenses or commissions others, those licensed or commissioned would then be able to perform substantially all of the religious functions of an ordained minister of the denomination and must do so on a regular, full-time basis.

As a commissioned or licensed unordained religious worker you do not qualify as a duly ordained, commissioned, or licensed minister of a church if you:

1) Are a member of a church or church denomination that provides for the ordination of ministers, and

2) Are *not* invested with the authority of an ordained minister.

Members of Religious Orders

A member of a religious order (except one who has taken a vow of poverty as a member of the order) is covered by social security under the self-employment provisions applying to the services performed in the capacity as a member. For the specific services covered, see *Services to Which Coverage or Exemption Applies*, discussed later.

If you are a member of a religious order who has taken a vow of poverty, you are automatically exempt from the payment of self-employment tax on amounts earned for services performed as an agent of your order and for your church or an integral agency thereof. However, if you are paid to perform services for an organization other than the church or an integral agency thereof, you are treated as a regular employee of the organization for federal employment tax purposes. The amounts earned are subject to federal income tax withholding, social security, and federal unemployment tax and are not considered self-employment income.

Vow-of-poverty members performing services for the church or an integral agency thereof may be covered under social security if the order (or an autonomous subdivision thereof) irrevocably elects coverage for its current and future vow-of-poverty members and its lay employees (or has made a previous election covering its lay employees irrevocable). The religious order, or autonomous subdivision, elects coverage for its vow-of-poverty members by filing Form SS-16, *Certificate of Election of Coverage Under the Federal Insurance Contributions Act*. This coverage may also be elected for a limited retroactive period (up to 20 calendar quarters before the quarter in which the election certificate is filed) for certain vow-of-poverty members.

Christian Science Practitioners and Readers

Christian Science practitioners are covered by social security under the self-employment provisions that apply to their profession as Christian Science reader-practitioners.

A **Christian Science practitioner** is an individual who is a member in good standing of the Mother Church, The First Church of Christ, Scientist, in Boston, Massachusetts, who practices healing according to the teachings of Christian Science. Christian Science practitioners are specifically exempted from licensing by state laws. Some Christian Science practitioners also do work as Christian Science teachers or lecturers. Income they receive as teachers or lecturers is treated in the same manner as income from their work as practitioners.

A **Christian Science reader** has the status of an ordained, commissioned, or licensed minister.

Religious Workers

If you are a religious worker who does not come within one of the classes already discussed, you are not entitled to social security coverage under the self-employment provisions that apply to members of the clergy.

Religious, charitable, and educational organizations. Employees of these and similar organizations generally are not covered by social security unless the organization elects to be covered by the Federal Insurance Contributions Act. The organization may do this by filing an election certificate, Form SS-15, *Certificate Electing Social Security Coverage Under the Federal Insurance Contributions Act*, with the appropriate Internal Revenue Service Center. The filing of Form SS-15 certifies that the organization wants to have its employees covered. If such an election certificate is filed, social security coverage is given to:

1) Those employees who sign Form SS-15a, *List to Accompany Certificate on Form SS-15 Electing Social Security Coverage Under the Federal Insurance Contributions Act*, which is submitted with the election certificate,

2) Those employees who sign Form SS-15a Supplement, *Amendment to List on Form SS-15a Under the Federal Insurance Contributions Act*, which is filed within 24 months after the calendar quarter in which the election certificate is filed, indicating desire for social security coverage, and

3) Those persons who become employees of the organization after the calendar quarter in which the election certificate is filed.

U.S. Citizens, Resident and Nonresident Aliens

Generally, social security coverage under the self-employment provisions for individuals who do not reside in the United States is limited to citizens or resident aliens of the United States. Nonresident aliens are not eligible for social security coverage under the self-employment provisions of the Internal Revenue Code.

Residents of Puerto Rico, the Virgin Islands, Guam, and American Samoa, who are not citizens of the United States, are not considered to be nonresident aliens for self-employment tax purposes. They are covered by social security, as discussed later under *Net Earnings from Self-Employment.*

Exemption from Social Security Coverage

If you elected social security coverage for tax years ending before 1968, under the laws then in effect, you will continue to be covered. You cannot apply for an exemption after electing to be covered.

Form 4361, *Application for Exemption from Self-Employment Tax for Use by Ministers, Members of Religious Orders and Christian Science Practitioners,* is filed to request exemption from social security coverage. This form includes a statement that, because of your religious principles, you are conscientiously opposed to accepting (for services performed as a member of the clergy) any public (governmental) insurance that makes payments in the event of death, disability, old age, or retirement, or makes payments toward the cost of, or provides services for, medical care, including the benefits of any insurance system established by the Social Security Act.

You do not have to be opposed to accepting public insurance for services you perform in a capacity other than as a minister, member of a religious order, or Christian Science practitioner.

If you file an application for exemption *solely for economic reasons,* you have not made a valid election. You must pay self-employment tax.

To be eligible for the exemption, a minister must be able to establish that the ordaining, commissioning, or licensing body qualifies as a tax-exempt religious organization. In addition, a minister must establish that the organization is a church or a convention or association of churches.

A member of the clergy also must meet either of the following two tests:

1) Religious principles test based on institutional principles and discipline of the particular religious denomination to which the individual belongs, or

2) Conscientious opposition test based on religious considerations of individual ministers, members of religious orders, and Christian Science practitioners (rather than opposition based on the general conscience of any such individuals).

Under either test, your opposition must be based on religious grounds.

Where to file. The application must be filed in triplicate with the Internal Revenue Service Center indicated in the instructions for Form 4361. If you have no legal residence in the United States, mail the application forms to the Internal Revenue Service Center, Philadelphia, PA 19255.

When to file. An application for exemption must be filed on or before one of the follow ing dates, whichever is later:

1) The due date, including extensions, for fil ing your tax return for your second tax year ending after 1967; or

2) The due date, including extensions, for fil ing your tax return for the second tax ye beginning after 1953 in which you have net earnings from self-employment of $40 or more, any part of which consists of pay ment—

   a) To you for the services you performed as a minister, or

   b) To you as a member of a religious order who has not taken the vow of pov erty for services you performed as required by the order, or

   c) For the services you performed as a Christian Science practitioner.

Example 1. Reverend Lawrence Jaeger, o dained in 1980 has net earnings as a clergy man of $400 or more in 1980 and 1981 He has until April 15, 1982, to file his application for exemption. However, if Reverend Jaeger does not receive an exemption by April 15, 1981, his self-employment tax for 1980 is d on or before that date.

The filing date stated in this example cov ers situations in which the clergyman has ne earnings as a clergyman (plus any other self employment earnings) of $400 or more in consecutive tax years. In some cases, the first and second years in which the clergyma has such earnings may not be consecutive tax years.

Example 2. Reverend Jaeger has less tha $400 of net earnings as a clergyman in 198 but does meet the $400 requirement in 198 and 1982. He has until April 15, 1983, to file his application for exemption. However, if Reverend Jaeger does not receive an exemp tion by April 15, 1981, his self-employment for 1980 is due on or before that date.

Example 3. In 1978 Reverend Moss was o dained a minister and had over $400 in net earnings from his services as a minister. In 1979 Reverend Moss opened a book store. He received $500 for his services as a minis ter in 1979, but his related expenses were more than $500. Therefore, he had no net i come from his services as a minister in 1979 In that year, his net self-employment earning from the book store were $500. In 1980 Rev erend Moss had net earnings of $100 from h self-employment as a minister and $350 net self-employment earnings from the book store. Because Reverend Moss had net ear ings from self-employment in 1978 and 1980 that were more than $400 and part of the earnings in each of those years was for his services as a minister, he must file his appli cation for exemption on or before the due date (including extensions) of his 1980 in come tax return.

ctive date of exemption. A valid and y filed exemption application, if applied, is effective for the first tax year after and for all following tax years in which have $400 or more of net earnings from employment, part of which is for services member of the clergy.

xample. Reverend Thomas Austin, ordered in 1979, has net income of $400 or e as a minister in 1979 and 1980. He files alid application for exemption on February 1980. If an exemption is granted, it is effective for 1979 and following years.

he exemption applies only to income from rices as a member of the clergy. It does apply to any other self-employment income or to wages.

mption irrevocable. Once an exemption social security coverage is approved it not be revoked.

he right of an individual to file an application for exemption ceases upon death. There- e, the surviving spouse, executor, or ministrator may not file an application for mption for a deceased member of the gy.

rvices to Which overage or xemption Applies

you are covered by social security or if have received an exemption from cover- e, the coverage or the exemption applies y to the services discussed here.

nisters

ervice you perform as a minister, priest, bi, etc., in the exercise of your ministry in- des the ministration of sacerdotal functions d conducting of religious worship. It also in- des the control, conduct, and maintenance religious organizations (including the reli- us boards, societies, and other integral encies of such organizations), under the thority of a religious body constituting a urch or church denomination.

The control, conduct, and maintenance of a igious organization relates to directing, anaging, or promoting the activities of the ganization. A religious organization is con- ered under the authority of a religious body nstituting a church or church denomination t is organized and dedicated to carrying t the tenets and principles of a faith ac- rding to either the requirements or sanc- ns governing the creation of institutions of e faith.

Your service as a minister in the conduct of igious worship or the ministration of sacer- tal functions is in the exercise of your min- y regardless of whether it is performed for religious organization.

Services you perform as a minister for an ganization that is neither a religious organi- tion nor operated as an integral agency of a religious organization are not in the exer- cise of your ministry unless such services are performed according to an assignment or designation by a religious body constituting your church.

However, the assigned or designated ser- vices must be of the kind that are ordinarily the duties of a minister and must be per- formed for, or on behalf of, the church by you as agent of the church.

Ordinarily, your services are not assigned or designated services for employment tax purposes if any of the following circum- stances are present:

1) The organization for which you perform the services did not arrange with your church for your services,

2) You are performing services for the or- ganization that other employees of the or- ganization who have not been so designated are performing, or

3) You performed the same services before and after the designation.

If a church pays any amount toward your obligation for your income tax or self-employ- ment tax, other than from your salary, this is additional income to you and must be in- cluded in your gross income and self-employ- ment income.

The writing of religious books or articles is considered to be in the exercise of your min- istry. The royalties or other income from the sale of books or articles qualify as self-em- ployment income.

Services you perform not in the exercise of your ministry. The discussions on social se- curity coverage and the exemption from cov- erage do not apply to any service you perform for an organization that is neither a religious organization nor operated as an inte- gral agency of a religious organization if you do not perform that service according to an assignment or designation by your ecclesiasti- cal superiors. In such cases, only the service you perform in the conduct of religious wor- ship or the ministration of sacerdotal func- tions is in the exercise of your ministry.

Service you perform as a duly ordained, commissioned, or licensed minister of a church while employed by the United States, or a state, or possession of the United States, or the District of Columbia, or a foreign gov- ernment, or a political subdivision of any of the foregoing, is not considered to be in the exercise of your ministry for these purposes. This is true even though the service may in- volve the ministration of sacerdotal functions or the conduct of religious worship.

For example, service performed by a chap- lain in the Armed Forces of the United States is considered to be performed by a commis- sioned officer in this capacity, and not by a minister in the exercise of the ministry.

Likewise, service performed by a minister in a government owned and operated hospital is not considered to be an exercise of the minis- try for federal employment tax purposes.

Members of Religious Orders

Services performed by you as a member of a religious order (not under a vow of poverty) in the exercise of duties required by the order include all duties that you are directed or re- quired to perform by your ecclesiastical supe- riors.

However, for employment outside the order to constitute the exercise of duties required by the order for employment tax purposes, the services you perform must be of the type that are ordinarily the duties of members of the order and must be performed as part of the duties that are required to be exercised for, or on behalf of, the religious order as its agent. Ordinarily, a religious order is not en- gaged in the performance of services as a principal when the legal relationship of em- ployer and employee exists between the member and a third party with respect to the performance of the services. This is true even if the member has taken a vow of poverty.

If a member of a religious order is directed to perform services for another agency of the supervising church, or an associated institu- tion, the member will be considered to be performing the services as an agent of the or- der.

Example. Mark Brown and Elizabeth Green are members of a religious order and have taken vows of poverty. All claims to their earnings from personal industry are re- nounced and belong to the order.

Mark is licensed as an attorney in Kansas and was instructed by the superiors of the or- der to get a job with a law firm in Kansas. Mark joined a law firm and, as he requested, the firm made the salary payments directly to the order.

Elizabeth is an experienced secretary and was instructed by the superiors of the order to accept salaried employment with the local business office of the church that exercises general administrative supervision over the or- der. Elizabeth took the job in the church's business office and gave all her earnings from the church to the order.

Mark's services are not services in the ex- ercise of duties required by the order and the amounts he earns are subject to federal in- come tax withholding, social security, and federal unemployment tax. Elizabeth's ser- vices are services performed in the exercise of duties required by the order.

Christian Science Practitioners and Readers

Social security coverage or the exemption from such coverage, as discussed earlier, ap- plies only to the services performed by a Christian Science practitioner or reader in the exercise of that profession.

Net Earnings from Self-Employment

Generally, net earnings from self-employ- ment mean the gross income from an individ-

3

ual's trade or business minus the allowable business deductions.

Members of the Clergy

If you are a duly ordained, commissioned, or licensed minister, or a member of a religious order and have not taken the vow of poverty, or a Christian Science practitioner, your net earnings from self-employment include the gross income earned from the exercise of your ministry, the exercise of the duties required of you by the order, or the exercise of your profession as a Christian Science practitioner, minus the deductions related to the gross income.

Related deductions include:

1) Employee business expenses reported on line 24, Form 1040 (also see *Living abroad,* later), and

2) Unreimbursed business expenses allowed only as an itemized deduction on Schedule A (Form 1040), *Itemized Deductions.*

In addition to salaries and fees for your ministerial services, your net earnings from self-employment include offerings for marriages, baptisms, funerals, masses, etc., minus the deductions reported on Schedule C (Form 1040) that are related to the income. If the offering is made to the church, it is not included in your net earnings.

Rental value or allowance. You must include in your net income for *self-employment tax purposes* the fair rental value of a parsonage furnished to you or the rental allowance paid to you. You must also include the value of meals and lodging furnished in connection with services you perform in the exercise of your ministry or as a member of the order, even though these amounts are excluded from gross income for income tax purposes.

A rental allowance paid to you as part of your compensation for your ministerial services, is excludable from your gross income to the extent that:

1) You use the compensation to rent or provide a home, and

2) The rental allowance does not exceed reasonable compensation for the services performed.

However, you must include the rental allowance in figuring your net earnings from self-employment.

A minister's surviving spouse will not be allowed to claim this exclusion from gross income unless the survivor also performs, or performed, ministerial services and the amount of the allowance is pay for those services.

If, as an ordained minister of the gospel, you own your own home and receive as part of your pay a rental allowance, you may exclude from gross income the smallest of the following:

1) The amount actually used to provide a home,

2) The amount officially designated as a rental allowance, or

3 The fair rental value of the home, including furnishings, and appurtenances, such as a garage, plus utilities.

Any rental allowance that is more than reasonable compensation or the fair rental value of the home plus utilities is includible in gross income.

Amounts you contributed as a minister to an annuity plan, set up for you by your church, that are not included in your gross income, are not taken into account in determining your net earnings from self-employment.

Living abroad. Certain foreign source earned income may be exempt from federal income tax if you are a U.S. citizen in a foreign country or U.S. possession. Publication 54, *Tax Guide for U.S. Citizens Abroad,* contains a complete discussion of the circumstances under which that income is exempt. You may get this free publication from the Office of International Operations, Internal Revenue Service, Washington, D.C. 20225, or from most U.S. Embassies or consulates.

If you are a U.S. citizen who is a duly ordained, commissioned, or licensed minister of a church, or a member of a religious order (other than one who has taken a vow of poverty) serving abroad and living in a foreign country, your net earnings from self-employment are figured under a special rule. Net earnings include income from the exercise of the ministry, or from the exercise of duties required by the religious order, determined without regard to the exclusion of income earned by employees in hardship area camps that may apply for income tax purposes.

If you qualify, you may be entitled to a deduction for excess foreign living costs. This deduction includes a cost-of-living differential, housing expenses, schooling expenses, home leave transportation expenses, and a hardship area amount. You are required to reduce your gross income from self-employment by any allowable excess foreign living cost deduction in arriving at net earnings. See Publication 54, *Tax Guide for U.S. Citizens Abroad.*

A resident alien minister who performs ministerial services outside the United States, for a religious denomination that has its corporate headquarters in the United States, is subject to self-employment tax on income earned within and outside the United States, unless the minister has received an exemption from social security coverage.

American Samoa, Guam, and the Virgin Islands are not considered possessions of the United States for self-employment tax purposes. Therefore, a U.S. citizen's income from the exercise of the ministry, the exercise of duties required by a religious order, or the exercise of the profession as a Christian Science practitioner on any of these islands is included in the computation of net earnings from self-employment.

Pension payments or retirement allowance a retired minister of a church receives for vices performed in the exercise of the min are not net earnings from self-employmen

Income tax withholding. Although a minis ter's salary for service *in the exercise of* ministry is not subject to income tax with holding, a minister may be able to enter in voluntary withholding agreement with an e ployer to cover any income and self-emplo ment tax that may be due.

Husband and Wife Missionary Team

If a husband and wife are both duly ordained, commissioned, or licensed ministe of a church, and are engaged under an agreement that each is to perform specific services for which they are paid jointly or separately, the self-employment income m be divided between them according to the agreement.

If the agreement is with the minister-hus band only and the minister-wife has no sp cific duties for which she is paid, amounts received for their services are included in the husband's self-employment income. If they divided the income for self-employme tax purposes, an amended return should b filed, showing the entire amount as self-en ployment income of the husband. He is su ject to the maximum limitation on self-employment income for each calendar yea

A minister-missionary's wife who is not a ordained, commissioned, or licensed as a minister of a church may file a claim for re fund of any self-employment tax paid in er for any years for which the statutory perio limitations on refunds has not expired (no mally, within 3 years from the time the ret was filed or 2 years from the time the tax paid, whichever is later). Her earnings, in case, should not be included in her husba self-employment income. If the wife receiv pay for performing services for the organiz tion, she may be an employee of the orga zation for social security (FICA) purposes even though she is not a minister.

Maximum Self-Employment Income

For 1980 the maximum self-employment come subject to social security tax is $25,900. If you had wages subject to soci security tax, the maximum self-employme income is $25,900 minus the amount of th wages. For example, you have $1,000 of wages subject to social security tax durin the tax year. Your self-employment incom could not be more than $24,900.

Optional Methods for Figuring Net Earnings from Self-Employment

You may be able to use an optional met for figuring your net earnings from *nonfar*

4

self-employment. If you have net earnings from farm self-employment, you may use the *farm optional method*. See Publication 533, *Self-Employment Tax*. If you have net earnings from both farm and nonfarm self-employment, you may qualify for both options. In general, the optional methods for figuring net earnings from self-employment are intended to permit continued coverage for social security self-employment tax purposes, even though your income for the tax year is low.

Nonfarm Optional Method

You may use the nonfarm optional method if

● Your actual net earnings from nonfarm self-employment are less than $1,600,

● Your net earnings from nonfarm self-employment are less than two-thirds of the sum of your gross income from all your nonfarm trades or businesses, and

● You are self-employed *on a regular basis.*

You are considered self-employed *on a regular basis* if you had actual net earnings from self-employment of $400 or more in at least 2 of the 3 consecutive tax years before the year that you elect to use this method.

You may *not* use the nonfarm optional method for more than 5 tax years during your lifetime.

If your gross income from all nonfarm trades and businesses is *less than* $2,400 and if your net earnings from your nonfarm self-employment are:

● Less than $1,600, and

● Less than two-thirds of your gross nonfarm profit, you may report two-thirds of the gross income from your nonfarm business as net earnings from self-employment.

If your gross income from all nonfarm trades and businesses is *more than* $2,400 and if your net earnings from nonfarm self-employment are:

● Less than $1,600, and

● Less than two-thirds of your gross nonfarm profit, you may report $1,600 as your net earnings from nonfarm self-employment.

For more information on self-employment and the farm and nonfarm optional methods, see Publication 533, *Self-Employment Tax.*

Tax Returns

Self-Employment Tax Returns

If you have not filed for and received an exemption from social security coverage for tax years after 1967, and have net earnings from self-employment of $400 or more in a tax year, as discussed under *Net Earnings from Self-Employment*, you must file an income tax return on Form 1040, even though you are not otherwise required to do so. Your self-employment tax is figured on Schedule SE (Form 1040).

For social security purposes, you figure your earnings from services as a member of the clergy as if you were self-employed, even though you may be performing those services as an employee.

Form 1040SS. Residents of the Virgin Islands, Guam, and American Samoa file Form 1040SS instead of Schedule SE. U.S. citizens residing in the Northern Mariana Islands on the last day of their tax year also must file Form 1040SS instead of Schedule SE.

Formulario 1040–PR. Residents of Puerto Rico who are not required to file a federal income tax return must file Formulario 1040–PR, or Form 1040SS if appropriate.

Rate of tax. For 1980 the self-employment tax rate is 8.1% on income up to $25,900.

Joint return. If you file a joint income tax return with your spouse and you both have self-employment income, you must each figure self-employment tax on your separate self-employment income, rather than on the sum of the two amounts. A separate Schedule SE must be filed by you and your spouse if you each have net self-employment income of at least $400. The computation of self-employment tax differs from the computation of income tax when a joint return is filed.

If one of you have net earnings of less than $400, those earnings are not subject to self-employment tax, even though you file a joint income tax return.

When to File Tax Returns

If you file your income tax return on the calendar year basis, the due date for filing the return is April 15 of the next year. If you are abroad on April 15, the time for filing your return is automatically extended to June 15.

If you file your return on the fiscal year basis, it is due by the 15th day of the fourth month of your next tax year. If you are abroad on that date, the time for filing is extended to the 15th day of the sixth month of your next tax year.

If the 15th day of the applicable month falls on a Saturday, Sunday, or holiday, you have until the first day after the 15th that is not a Saturday, Sunday, or holiday.

If you take advantage of the extension, you must attach a statement to your return showing you were residing or traveling outside the United States on the due date. You must pay interest on the unpaid tax from the due date (April 15 if you file on the calendar year basis) until paid.

If you live in the United States, you may receive an extension for filing your return. This is done by filing Form 4868, *Application for Automatic Extension of Time to File U.S. Individual Income Tax Return*. The application must be filed, on or before the due date of the return, with the Internal Revenue Service Center for your area.

Note. Your return is timely filed if it bears an official postmark dated no later than midnight of the last date for filing, including any extensions.

Where to File Tax Returns

Form 1040. If you live in a foreign country or a U.S. possession, other than permanent residents of the Virgin Islands who have no legal residence or place of business in the United States and residents of Guam or the Northern Mariana Islands on the last day of their tax year, you should file your return with the Internal Revenue Service Center, Philadelphia, PA 19255. Those who are not certain of the place of their legal residence and who have no principal place of business in the United States may also file with the Internal Revenue Service Center in Philadelphia.

If you are a resident of Guam on the last day of your tax year, file your income tax return with the Commissioner of Revenue and Taxation, Agaña, Guam 96910.

If you are a resident of the Northern Mariana Islands on the last day of your tax year, file your return with the U.S. Internal Revenue Service, Saipan, Mariana Islands 96950.

If you are a permanent resident of the Virgin Islands, you should file your return with the Department of Finance, Tax Division, Charlotte Amalie, St. Thomas. Virgin Islands 00801, even though your legal residence or principal place of business is located in the United States. However, if you are not a permanent resident of the Virgin Islands but maintain your legal residence or principal place of business there, you should file your return with the Internal Revenue Service Center, Philadelphia, PA 19255.

All others file according to instructions relating to preparation of Form 1040.

Formulario 1040–PR and Form 1040SS. Taxpayers living in Puerto Rico, Guam, or in U.S. possessions should file with the Internal Revenue Service Center, Philadelphia, PA 19255.

Declaration of Estimated Tax

If you are a member of the clergy, you must file a declaration of estimated tax on Form 1040–ES and pay the estimated tax or the first installment by April 15 of any year in which you expect to owe income tax and self-employment tax of $100 or more. However, if you are abroad on April 15, the time for filing the declaration is automatically extended to June 15.

For more information on estimated tax, see Publication 505, *Tax Withholding and Estimated Tax*

Retirement Savings Arrangements

Keogh (H.R.10) plans. Although ministers, members of religious orders, Christian Science practitioners and readers, and certain other common-law employees may treat their pay for services rendered as earnings from self-employment for social security purposes, this does not necessarily establish that they are self-employed for the purpose of participation in a qualified retirement plan that includes self-employed individuals.

For example, a minister employed by a congregation on a salaried basis is a common-law employee, not a self-employed individual, even though for social security purposes compensation is treated as net earnings from self-employment. On the other hand, amounts received directly from members of the congregation, such as fees for performing marriages, baptisms, or other personal services, represent earnings from self-employment.

Whether a particular individual is a common-law employee or is self-employed depends on all the facts and circumstances. For example, doctors of medicine and Christian Science practitioners are treated as being self-employed if they are not, in fact, common-law employees.

For more information on establishing a Keogh (H.R.10) plan, see Publication 560, *Tax Information on Self-Employed Retirement Plans.*

Individual retirement arrangements (IRA's). You may establish your own IRA if you are not covered under a qualified retirement plan (including H.R.10, government, or tax-exempt organization annuity plans).

You are allowed to make contributions to this program equal to 15% of your pay, or $1,500 each year, whichever is less. Contributions made to such a program generally are tax deductible. This will create a fund from which you will receive income during your retirement years. Income earned by the fund will not be taxable until it is distributed to you.

Publication 590, *Tax Information on Individual Retirement Arrangements,* discusses the general provisions for establishing an individual retirement arrangement, the types of programs available, and the filing requirements once a program is established.

Comprehensive Example

Reverend Abner Hale is the minister of the First United Church. He is an employee of the church. The Reverend has not applied for an exemption from social security coverage. The church paid Reverend Hale a salary of $11,510 during the year. Reverend Hale made estimated tax payments totaling $3,300 during the year. The Reverend lives in the church's parsonage that has a fair rental value of $250 a month. The church separately paid Reverend Hale $100 a month for utility costs for the parsonage. Reverend Hale's utility bills averaged $80 a month. Even though the church does not withhold FICA taxes or federal income taxes (because Reverend Hale has not requested voluntary withholding of income tax), the church reports his salary on Form W–2. The W–2 that the Reverend received from the church shows the $11,510 as wages, tips, and other compensation. In addition to his salary, the Reverend received $1,900 during the year for weddings, baptisms, and honoraria that was not earned in his capacity as an employee of the church.

On Form 1040, illustrated later, Reverend Hale reports his salary of $11,510 plus $240, the excess utility allowance over utility costs. He deducts $600 for the 3,000 miles he used his car for his services as an employee of the church. The fair rental value of the parsonage is not included in income for income tax purposes.

The Reverend spent $47 during the year for magazines and books that he used in connection with his services as an employee of the church. The church did not repay him. The $47 may only be deducted as an itemized deduction on Schedule A (Form 1040). However, the Reverend does not file Schedule A to deduct the $47 because his itemized deductions are not more than his zero bracket amount of $2,300.

On Schedule C (Form 1040) Reverend Hale reports the $1,900 from weddings, baptisms, and honoraria. The Reverend's related expenses for the year were $55 for marriage and family booklets and $140 for 700 miles of business use of his automobile figured at the standard mileage rate of 20¢ a mile (mainly trips in connection with honoraria).

On Schedule SE (Form 1040) the Reverend *does* include the fair rental value of the parsonage ($3,000) plus his other income, including the entire $100 a month utility allowance, minus $600 for mileage expenses for regular church business. In addition, he deducts the $47 he paid for the books and magazines on Line 7.

Form **1040** Department of the Treasury—Internal Revenue Service
U.S. Individual Income Tax Return **1980**

| For Privacy Act Notice, see Instructions | For the year January 1–December 31, 1980, or other tax year beginning | 1980, ending | 19 |

Use IRS label. Otherwise, please print or type.

Your first name and initial (if joint return, also give spouse's name and initial) **Abner** Last name **Hale** Your social security number **462 62 6594**

Present home address (Number and street, including apartment number, or rural route) **801 Main Street** Spouse's social security no.

City, town or post office, State and ZIP code **Anytown, Texas 77859** Your occupation ▶ **Minister** Spouse's occupation ▶

Presidential Election Campaign Fund
Do you want $1 to go to this fund? . . . . ✔ Yes ☐ No
If joint return, does your spouse want $1 to go to this fund? . . . Yes ☐ No
Note: Checking "Yes" will not increase your tax or reduce your refund.

Requested by Census Bureau for Revenue Sharing
A Where do you live (actual location of residence)? (See page 2 of Instructions.) State: **TX** City, village, borough, etc. **Anytown**
B Do you live within the legal limits of a city, village, etc.? ☐ Yes ☑ No
C In what county do you live? **Town**
D In what township do you live?

Filing Status
Check only one box.

1 ✔ Single
2 ☐ Married filing joint return (even if only one had income)
3 ☐ Married filing separate return. Enter spouse's social security no. above and full name here ▶
4 ☐ Head of household. (See page 6 of Instructions.) If qualifying person is your unmarried child, enter child's name ▶
5 ☐ Qualifying widow(er) with dependent child (Year spouse died ▶ 19   ). (See page 6 of Instructions.)

Exemptions
Always check the box labeled Yourself. Check other boxes if they apply.

6a ✔ Yourself ☐ 65 or over ☐ Blind
b ☐ Spouse ☐ 65 or over ☐ Blind
Enter number of boxes checked on 6a and b ▶ **1**

c First names of your dependent children who lived with you ▶
Enter number of children listed on 6c ▶

d Other dependents: (1) Name	(2) Relationship	(3) Number of months lived in your home	(4) Did dependent have income of $1,000 or more?	(5) Did you provide more than one-half of dependent's support?

Enter number of other dependents ▶

7 Total number of exemptions claimed . . . .
Add numbers entered in boxes above ▶ **1**

Income
Please attach Copy B of your Forms W–2 here.
If you do not have a W–2, see page 5 of Instructions.

8	Wages, salaries, tips, etc.	8	11,510 00
9	Interest income (attach Schedule B if over $400)	9	
10a	Dividends (attach Schedule B if over $400) . . . . . 10b Exclusion		
c	Subtract line 10b from line 10a	10c	
11	Refunds of State and local income taxes (do not enter an amount unless you deducted those taxes in an earlier year—see page 9 of Instructions)	11	
12	Alimony received	12	
13	Business income or (loss) (attach Schedule C)	13	1,705 00
14	Capital gain or (loss) (attach Schedule D)	14	
15	40% of capital gain distributions not reported on line 14 (See page 9 of Instructions) .	15	
16	Supplemental gains or (losses) (attach Form 4797)	16	
17	Fully taxable pensions and annuities not reported on line 18	17	
18	Pensions, annuities, rents, royalties, partnerships, etc. (attach Schedule E) . . .	18	
19	Farm income or (loss) (attach Schedule F)	19	
20a	Unemployment compensation (insurance). Total received	20b	
b	Taxable amount, if any, from worksheet on page 10 of Instructions		
21	Other income (state nature and source—see page 10 of Instructions) ▶ **Excess Utility Allowance**	21	240 00
22	Total income. Add amounts in column for lines 8 through 21 . . . . ▶	22	13,455 00

Please attach check or money order here.

Adjustments to Income
(See Instructions on page 10)

23	Moving expense (attach Form 3903 or 3903F)	23		
24	Employee business expenses (attach Form 2106) . .	24	600 00	
25	Payments to an IRA (enter code from page 10 . . . .) .	25		
26	Payments to a Keogh (H.R. 10) retirement plan . .	26		
27	Interest penalty on early withdrawal of savings . . .	27		
28	Alimony paid	28		
29	Disability income exclusion (attach Form 2440) . .	29		
30	Total adjustments. Add lines 23 through 29		30	600 00

Adjusted Gross Income

31 Adjusted gross income. Subtract line 30 from line 22. If this line is less than $10,000, see "Earned Income Credit" (line 57) on pages 13 and 14 of Instructions. If you want IRS to figure your tax, see page 3 of Instructions . . . . . ▶ | 31 | 12,855 00 |

Form **1040** (1980)

7

Form 1040 (1980)   Page 2

Tax Computation (See Instructions on page 11)	32 Amount from line 31 *(adjusted gross income)*	32	12,855 00
	33 If you do not itemize deductions, enter zero . . . . } If you itemize, complete Schedule A (Form 1040) and enter the amount from Schedule A, line 41 . . .	33	-0-
	Caution: If you have unearned income and can be claimed as a dependent on your parent's return, check here ▶ ☐ and see page 11 of the Instructions. Also see page 11 of the Instructions if: • You are married filing a separate return and your spouse itemizes deductions, OR • You file Form 4563, OR • You are a dual-status alien.		
	34 Subtract line 33 from line 32. Use the amount on line 34 to find your tax from the Tax Tables, or to figure your tax on Schedule TC, Part I . . . . Use Schedule TC, Part I, and the Tax Rate Schedules ONLY if: • Line 34 is more than $20,000 ($40,000 if you checked Filing Status Box 2 or 5), OR • You have more exemptions than are shown in the Tax Table for your filing status, OR • You use Schedule G or Form 4726 to figure your tax. Otherwise, you MUST use the Tax Tables to find your tax.	34	12,855 00
	35 Tax. Enter tax here and check if from ☑ Tax Tables or ☐ Schedule TC	35	1,813 00
	36 Additional taxes. (See page 12 of Instructions.) Enter here and check if from ☐ Form 4970, ☐ Form 4972, ☐ Form 5544, ☐ Form 5405, or ☐ Section 72(m)(5) penalty tax . . }	36	
	37 **Total.** Add lines 35 and 36 . . . . ▶	37	1,813 00
Credits (See Instructions on page 12)	38 Credit for contributions to candidates for public office . . .	38		
	39 Credit for the elderly *(attach Schedules R&RP)*	39		
	40 Credit for child and dependent care expenses *(attach Form 2441)*	40		
	41 Investment credit *(attach Form 3468)*	41		
	42 Foreign tax credit *(attach Form 1116)*	42		
	43 Work incentive (WIN) credit *(attach Form 4874)*	43		
	44 Jobs credit *(attach Form 5884)*	44		
	45 Residential energy credits *(attach Form 5695)*	45		
	46 Total credits. Add lines 38 through 45	46	
	47 Balance. Subtract line 46 from line 37 and enter difference (but not less than zero) . ▶	47	1,813 00
Other Taxes (Including Advance EIC Payments)	48 Self-employment tax *(attach Schedule SE)*	48	1,358 00
	49a Minimum tax. Attach Form 4625 and check here ▶ ☐	49a	
	49b Alternative minimum tax. Attach Form 6251 and check here ▶ ☐	49b	
	50 Tax from recomputing prior-year investment credit *(attach Form 4255)*	50	
	51a Social security (FICA) tax on tip income not reported to employer *(attach Form 4137)* . .	51a	
	51b Uncollected employee FICA and RRTA tax on tips *(from Form W-2)*	51b	
	52 Tax on an IRA *(attach Form 5329)*	52	
	53 Advance earned income credit (EIC) payments received *(from Form W-2)*	53	
	54 **Balance.** Add lines 47 through 53 . . . . ▶	54	3,171 00
Payments Attach Forms W-2, W-2G, and W-2P to front.	55 Total Federal income tax withheld	55		
	56 1980 estimated tax payments and amount applied from 1979 return .	56	3,300 00	
	57 Earned income credit. If line 32 is under $10,000, see pages 13 and 14 of Instructions	57		
	58 Amount paid with Form 4868	58		
	59 Excess FICA and RRTA tax withheld (two or more employers)	59		
	60 Credit for Federal tax on special fuels and oils *(attach Form 4136 or 4136-T)*	60		
	61 Regulated Investment Company credit *(attach Form 2439)*	61		
	62 **Total.** Add lines 55 through 61 . . . . ▶	62	3,300 00
Refund or Balance Due	63 If line 62 is larger than line 54, enter amount **OVERPAID** . . . . ▶	63	129 00
	64 Amount of line 63 to be **REFUNDED TO YOU** . . . . ▶	64	
	65 Amount of line 63 to be applied to your 1981 estimated tax . . . ▶	65	129 00	
	66 If line 54 is larger than line 62, enter **BALANCE DUE.** Attach check or money order for full amount payable to "Internal Revenue Service." Write your social security number on check or money order . . ▶ (Check ▶ ☐ if Form 2210 (2210F) is attached. See page 15 of Instructions.) ▶ $	66	
Please Sign Here	Under penalties of perjury, I declare that I have examined this return, including accompanying schedules and statements, and to the best of my knowledge and belief, it is true, correct, and complete. Declaration of preparer (other than taxpayer) is based on all information of which preparer has any knowledge. ▶ *Abner Hale* ▶ *March 12, 1981* ▶ Your signature Date Spouse's signature (if filing jointly, BOTH must sign even if only one had income)		
Paid Preparer's Use Only	Preparer's signature and date ▶	Check if self-employed ▶ ☐	Preparer's social security no.
	Firm's name (or yours, if self-employed) ▶ and address	E.I. No. ▶ ZIP code ▶	

8

SCHEDULE C (Form 1040) Department of the Treasury Internal Revenue Service	**Profit or (Loss) From Business or Profession** (Sole Proprietorship) Partnerships, Joint Ventures, etc., Must File Form 1065. ► Attach to Form 1040 or Form 1041. ► See Instructions for Schedule C (Form 1040).	**1980** 09

Name of proprietor Abner Hale	Social security number of proprietor 462 62 6594

A Main business activity (see Instructions) ► Minister   ; product ► Service

B Business name ► First United Church

C Employer identification number

D Business address (number and street) ► 800 Main Street
City, State and ZIP Code ► Anytown, Texas 77859

E Accounting method: (1) ☑ Cash   (2) ☐ Accrual   (3) ☐ Other (specify) ► ....

C

F Method(s) used to value closing inventory:
(1) ☐ Cost   (2) ☐ Lower of cost or market   (3) ☐ Other (if other, attach explanation)

	Yes	No
G Was there any major change in determining quantities, costs, or valuations between opening and closing inventory? If "Yes," attach explanation.		
H Did you deduct expenses for an office in your home?		✓
I Did you elect to claim amortization (under section 191) or depreciation (under section 167(o)) for a rehabilitated certified historic structure (see Instructions)? (Amortizable basis (see Instructions) ►		

Part I   Income

1 a Gross receipts or sales		**1a**		
b Returns and allowances		**1b**		
c Balance (subtract line 1b from line 1a)		**1c**		
2 Cost of goods sold and/or operations (Schedule C–1, line 8)		**2**		
3 Gross profit (subtract line 2 from line 1c)		**3**		
4 Other income (attach schedule) $1,900. offerings for marriages, baptisms, and honoraria		**4**	1,900	00
5 Total income (add lines 3 and 4) ►		**5**	1,900	00

Part II   Deductions

6 Advertising		**31 a** Wages		
7 Amortization		**b** Jobs credit		
8 Bad debts from sales or services		**c** WIN credit		
9 Bank charges		**d** Total credits		
10 Car and truck expenses		**e** Subtract line 31d from 31a		
11 Commissions		**32** Other expenses (specify):		
12 Depletion		**a** Marriage + family booklets	55	00
13 Depreciation (explain in Schedule C–2)		**b** Car - 900 mi @ 20 ¢	140	00
14 Dues and publications		**c**		
15 Employee benefit programs		**d**		
16 Freight (not included on Schedule C–1)		**e**		
17 Insurance		**f**		
18 Interest on business indebtedness		**g**		
19 Laundry and cleaning		**h**		
20 Legal and professional services		**i**		
21 Office supplies		**j**		
22 Pension and profit-sharing plans		**k**		
23 Postage		**l**		
24 Rent on business property		**m**		
25 Repairs		**n**		
26 Supplies (not included on Schedule C–1)		**o**		
27 Taxes		**p**		
28 Telephone		**q**		
29 Travel and entertainment		**r**		
30 Utilities		**s**		

33 Total deductions (add amounts in columns for lines 6 through 32s) ►	**33**	195	00
34 Net profit or (loss) (subtract line 33 from line 5). If a profit, enter on Form 1040, line 13, and on Schedule SE, Part II, line 5a (or Form 1041, line 6). If a loss, go on to line 35.	**34**	1,705	00

35 If you have a loss, do you have amounts for which you are not "at risk" in this business (see Instructions)? ☐ Yes ☐ No

9

SCHEDULE SE (Form 1040) Department of the Treasury Internal Revenue Service	**Computation of Social Security Self-Employment Tax** ▶ See Instructions for Schedule SE (Form 1040). ▶ Attach to Form 1040.	19**80** 23

Name of self-employed person (as shown on social security card) Abner Hale	Social security number of self-employed person ▶	462 62 6594

Part I Computation of Net Earnings from FARM Self-Employment

Regular Method

1 Net profit or (loss) from:

a Schedule F (Form 1040)	1a		
b Farm partnerships	1b		
2 Net earnings from farm self-employment (add lines 1a and 1b)	2		

Farm Optional Method

3 If gross profits from farming are:

a Not more than $2,400, enter two-thirds of the gross profits . . . . }	3		
b More than $2,400 and the net farm profit is less than $1,600, enter $1,600			

4 Enter here and on line 12a, the amount on line 2, or line 3 if you elect the farm optional method .	4		

Part II Computation of Net Earnings from NONFARM Self-Employment **SE**

Regular Method

5 Net profit or (loss) from:

a Schedule C (Form 1040)	5a	1,705	00
b Partnerships, joint ventures, etc. (other than farming)	5b		
c Service as a minister, member of a religious order, or a Christian Science practitioner. (Include rental value of parsonage or rental allowance furnished.) If you filed Form 4361 and have not revoked that exemption, check here ▶ ☐ and enter zero on this line	5c	15,110	00 ²⁾
d Service with a foreign government or international organization	5d		
e Other (specify) ▶	5e		
6 Total (add lines 5a through 5e)	6	16,815	00
7 Enter adjustments if any (attach statement, see page 29 of Instructions)	7	< 47 00> ²⁾	
8 Adjusted net earnings or (loss) from nonfarm self-employment (line 6, as adjusted by line 7) . .	8	16,768	00

Note: *If line 8 is $1,600 or more or if you do not elect to use the Nonfarm Optional Method, skip lines 9 through 11 and enter amount from line 8 on line 12b.*

Nonfarm Optional Method

9 Maximum amount reportable under both optional methods combined (farm and nonfarm) . .	9a	$1,600	00
b Enter amount from line 3. (If you did not elect to use the farm optional method, enter zero.) .	9b		
c Balance (subtract line 9b from line 9a)	9c		
10 Enter two-thirds of gross nonfarm profits or $1,600, whichever is smaller	10		
11 Enter here and on line 12b, the amount on line 9c or line 10, whichever is smaller	11		

Part III Computation of Social Security Self-Employment Tax

12 Net earnings or (loss):

a From farming (from line 4)	12a		
b From nonfarm (from line 8, or line 11 if you elect to use the Nonfarm Optional Method) . .	12b	16,768	00
13 Total net earnings or (loss) from self-employment reported on lines 12a and 12b. (If line 13 is less than $400, you are not subject to self-employment tax. Do not fill in rest of schedule)	13	16,768	00
14 The largest amount of combined wages and self-employment earnings subject to social security or railroad retirement taxes for 1980 is	14	$25,900	00

15 a Total "FICA" wages (from Forms W–2) and "RRTA" compensation	15a				
b Unreported tips subject to FICA tax from Form 4137, line 9 or to RRTA	15b				

c Add lines 15a and 15b	15c	– 0 –	
16 Balance (subtract line 15c from line 14)	16	25,900	00
17 Self-employment income—line 13 or 16, whichever is smaller	17	16,768	00
18 Self-employment tax. (If line 17 is $25,900, enter $2,097.90; if less, multiply the amount on line 17 by .081.) Enter here and on Form 1040, line 48	18	1,358	00

1) Salary of $11,510 minus $600.00 mileage for church business (3,000 mi @ 20¢) $3,000.00
rental value of parsonage + $1,200 utility allowance = $15,110.

2) Unreimbursed expenses - Books and magazines $47.00

10

4361	**Application for Exemption from Self-Employment Tax for Use by Ministers, Members of Religious Orders and Christian Science Practitioners**	**File in Triplicate with Internal Revenue Service**

. May 1980)
tment of the Treasury
nal Revenue Service

Documentation required by Specific Instruction Item 4 MUST be attached to this form. Before filing this form see General Instructions.

1 Name	2 Social security number

Address

City or town, State and ZIP code

heck ONLY ONE box: ☐ Christian Science practitioner ☐ Ordained minister, priest, rabbi ☐ Member of religious order not under a vow of poverty ☐ Commissioned or licensed minister (see Item 7)	4 Date ordained, licensed, etc.

egal name of ordaining, licensing, or commissioning body or religious order	Employer identification number

ddress

ity or town, State and ZIP code

nter the first two years after the date entered in Item 4, above, in which you had net earnings from self-employ-
ent of $400 or more, some part of which was from services as a minister, priest, rabbi, etc.; or as a member of
religious order; or as a Christian Science practitioner . . . . ▶ | 19 | 19 |

tion: Form 4361 is not proof of any of the following: (a) the right to an exemption from Federal income tax withholding and social security tax; (b) the right to a parsonage allowance exclusion (section 107 of the Internal Revenue Code); or (c) assignment by your religious superiors to a particular job.

certify that, because of my religious principles, I am conscientiously opposed to the acceptance (with respect to services performed by me as a minister, member, or practitioner) of the benefits of any public insurance that makes payments in the event of death, disability, old-age, or retirement or makes payments toward the cost of, or provides services for, medical care (including the benefits of any insurance system established by the Social Security Act).

certify that I did not file an effective waiver certificate (Form 2031) electing social security coverage on earnings as a minister, member, or practitioner.

hereby request an exemption from payment of self-employment tax with respect to my earnings from services as a ▸minister, member, or practitioner, pursuant to the provisions of section 1402(e) of the Internal Revenue Code. I understand that the exemption, if granted, will apply only to such earnings. Under penalties of perjury, I declare that this application has been examined by me and to the best of my knowledge and belief it is true and correct.

ature ▶   Date ▶

: The exemption is granted only if the application is approved by Internal Revenue Service, and Copy C is returned to you marked "approved."

For Internal Revenue Service Use	COPY A
Approved for exemption from self-employment tax (see Caution above) Disapproved for exemption from self-employment tax	To be retained by Internal Revenue Service
.... (Director's signature) .... (Date)	

eral Instructions

you are a member of a religious order who
taken a vow of poverty, do not file this form
use you are automatically exempt from the
nent of self-employment tax for amounts
ed for services performed for your church
n integral agency thereof. However, members
religious order who are under a vow of pov-
and are paid to perform services for an
nization other than the church or an integral
cy of it are treated as regular employees of
organization for Federal employment tax
oses (Federal income tax withholding, social
rity and Federal unemployment tax). The
matic exemption from self-employment tax
not apply to amounts earned during such
loyment.

. **Purpose of This Form.**—This form
uld be used to request exemption under
Self-Employment Contributions Act for
ices performed by a minister, member
 religious order, or Christian Science
titioner.

Who May File for Exemption.—Any

duly ordained, commissioned, or licensed minister of a church, member of a religious order (who has not taken the vow of poverty), or Christian Science practitioner may file for exemption from self-employment tax. To be eligible for the exemption, the applicant must establish that the ordaining, commissioning, or licensing body (or religious order) is a church that is exempt from Federal income tax under section 501(a) of the Internal Revenue Code as a religious organization described in section 501(c)(3), and must also establish that the church (or convention or association of churches) is one described in section 170(b)(1)(A)(i). The request must be based on a conscientious opposition, because of the applicant's religious principles, to accepting (for services performed as a minister, member, or practitioner) public insurance (including social security benefits) that makes payments in the event of death, disability, old-age, or retirement or makes payments toward the cost of, or provides services for, medical care. However, if the minister, member, or practitioner has previously filed an effective waiver certificate Form 2031, an exemption may NOT now be filed.

Commissioned or licensed ministers of a church or church denomination that provides for ordination of ministers may file an application for exemption if they are invested with the authority to perform substantially all of the religious duties of their church or church denomination.

For more information, see Publication 517, Social Security for Members of the Clergy and Religious Workers.

C. Earnings to Which This Exemption Applies.—An exemption that is effective for a duly ordained, commissioned, or licensed minister of a church applies only to service performed in the exercise of the ministry.

Service performed by a minister in the exercise of the ministry includes the ministration of sacerdotal functions, the conduct of religious worship, and the control, conduct, and maintenance of religious organizations (including the religious boards, societies, and other integral agencies of such organizations), under the authority of a religious body constituting a church or church denomination. The following rules apply in determining whether services performed by a minister are performed in the exercise of the ministry.

(Continued on back)

Form **4361** (Rev. 5–80)

If a minister is performing service in the conduct of religious worship or the ministration of sacerdotal functions, this service is in the exercise of the ministry whether or not it is performed for a religious organization.

If a minister is performing service for an organization that operates as an integral agency of a religious organization under the authority of a religious body constituting a church or church denomination, all service performed by the minister in the conduct of religious worship, in the ministration of sacerdotal functions, or in the control, conduct, and maintenance of such organization is in the exercise of the ministry. The following example illustrates this rule:

Example: M, a duly ordained minister, is engaged by the N Religious Board to serve as director of one of its departments. M performs no other service. The N Religious Board is an integral agency of O, a religious organization operating under the authority of a religious body constituting a church denomination. M is performing service in the exercise of M's ministry.

If a minister, under an assignment or designation by a religious body constituting the minister's church, performs service for an organization that is neither a religious organization nor operated as an integral agency of a religious organization, all service performed by the minister, even though this service may not involve the conduct of religious worship or the ministration of sacerdotal functions, is in the exercise of the ministry. Ordinarily, the services of a minister are not assigned or designated services if any of the following circumstances are present: (1) the organization for which the minister performs the services did not arrange with the minister's church for the minister's services; (2) the minister is performing services for the organization that other employees of the organization who have not been so designated are performing; or (3) the minister performed the same services before and after the designation.

D. Earnings to Which This Exemption Does Not Apply.—An exemption that is effective for a duly ordained, commissioned, or licensed minister of a church does not apply to service performed that is not in the exercise of the ministry.

If a minister is performing service for an organization that is neither a religious organization nor operated as an integral agency of a religious organization and the service is not performed under an assignment or designation by the minister's ecclesiastical superiors, then only the service performed by the minister in the conduct of religious worship or the ministration of sacerdotal functions is in the exercise of the ministry. The following example illustrates this rule:

Example: M, a duly ordained minister, is engaged by N University to teach history and mathematics. M performs no other service for N although from time to time M performs marriages and conducts funerals for relatives and friends. N University is neither a religious organization nor operated as an integral agency of a religious organization. M is not performing the service for N under an assignment or designation by M's ecclesiastical superiors. The service performed by M for N University is not in the exercise of M's ministry. However, service performed by M in performing marriages and conducting funerals is in the exercise of M's ministry.

Service performed by a duly ordained, commissioned, or licensed minister of a church as an employee of the United States, or a State, territory, or possession of the United States, or the District of Columbia, or a foreign government, or a political subdivision of any of the foregoing, is not considered to be in the exercise of the ministry for purposes of the tax on self-employment income, even though this service may involve the ministration of sacerdotal functions or the conduct of religious worship. For example, service performed by a chaplain in the Armed Forces of the United States is considered to be performed by a commissioned officer in this capacity and not by a minister in the exercise of the ministry. Similarly, service performed by a chaplain in a State prison or State University is considered to be performed by a civil servant of the State and not by a minister in the exercise of the ministry.

E. Time Limitation for Filing Application for Exemption.—An application for exemption must be filed with the Internal Revenue Service by the later of the two following dates: (1) the due date of your tax return (including extensions) for the second tax year in which you have net earnings from self-employment of $400 or more, any part of which was derived from services as a minister, member of a religious order or Christian Science practitioner; or (2) the due date (including extensions) of your tax return for your second tax year ending after 1967.

Example: Reverend Aker, ordained in 1965, had net ministerial earnings of $400 or more in all years after 1965 and had not filed a waiver certificate electing social security coverage (Form 2031). He should have filed an application for exemption by April 15, 1970, or extended date.

Reverend Beeker, ordained in 1977, had ministerial income of $400 or more in 1977 and in 1978. He may file an application for exemption not later than April 16, 1979, or extended date.

F. Effective Date of Exemption.—An exemption from self-employment tax is effective for the first tax year ending after 1967, and all succeeding tax years in which you have net earnings from self-employment of $400 or more, any part of which is derived from services as a minister, member, or practitioner. Thus, if you had qualified net earnings of $400 or more in 1968 and 1979, a valid application for exemption from self-employment tax filed by April 15, 1980, would be effective for 1968 and all years thereafter. However, contact an IRS office to see if you are entitled to file a claim for refund of self-employment taxes paid in prior tax years.

G. Where to File.—Mail your application to the Internal Revenue Service Center for the place where you live.

New Jersey, New York City and counties of Nassau, Rockland, Suffolk, and Westchester	Holtsville, NY 00501
New York (all other counties), Connecticut, Maine, Massachusetts, New Hampshire, Rhode Island, Vermont	Andover, MA 05501
Alabama, Florida, Georgia, Mississippi, South Carolina	Atlanta, GA 31101
Michigan, Ohio	Cincinnati, OH 45999
Louisiana, New Mexico, Arkansas, Kansas, Oklahoma, Texas	Austin, TX 73301
Alaska, Arizona, Colorado, Idaho, Minnesota, Montana, Nebraska, Nevada, North Dakota, Oregon, South Dakota, Utah, Washington, Wyoming	Ogden, UT 84201
Illinois, Iowa, Missouri, Wisconsin	Kansas City, MO 64999
California, Hawaii	Fresno, CA 93888
Indiana, Kentucky, North Carolina, Tennessee, Virginia, West Virginia	Memphis, TN 37501
Delaware, District of Columbia, Maryland, Pennsylvania	Philadelphia, PA 19255

If you have no legal residence in the United States then mail this form to the Internal Revenue Service Center, Philadelphia, PA 19255.

H. Extensions of Time for Filing and Noncalendar Year Taxpayers.—In general, the filing dates stated do not apply if you file your tax return other than for a calendar year or you are granted an extension of time to file your return. Contact the nearest Internal Revenue Service office for applicable dates.

I. How to Indicate Exemption on Form 1040.—If your only income subject to self-employment tax is from ministerial services, and Copy C has been returned to you approved by the Internal Revenue Service, write "Exempt-Form 4361" on the self-employment line in Other Taxes section of Form 1040. However, if you have other income subject to self-employment tax, see Schedule SE (Form 1040).

J. Revocation of Exemption.—You may not revoke the exemption once it is received.

Specific Instructions

Item 2.—Enter your social security number as it appears on your social security card. If you have no number, file application Form SS-5 with the local office of the Social Security Administration. If you do not receive your card in time, file Form 4361 and enter "Applied for" in the space provided for the number.

Item 4.—Enter the date you were duly ordained, commissioned, or licensed as a minister of a church, or date you became a member of a religious order, or date you commenced practice as a Christian Science practitioner. No application for exemption should be filed prior to this date. A copy of the certificate (or a letter from the governing body of your church if you did not receive a certificate) establishing your status as a duly ordained, commissioned, or a licensed minister, or member of religious order, or Christian Science practitioner must be attached to the form.

Item 5.—If you are a minister or a member of a religious order, enter the legal name, address, and employer identification number of the church denomination that ordained, commissioned, or licensed you or the order of which you are now a member. The employer identification number should be obtained from the ordaining, licensing, or commissioning body or religious order.

1040-ES | Department of the Treasury—Internal Revenue Service
Declaration of Estimated Tax for Individuals | 1981

structions

Note: In general, "estimated tax" is the ount of tax you owe that for some reason was withheld from your pay. In general, you do have to file a declaration of estimated tax if ur 1981 income tax return will show (1) a tax ind or (2) a tax balance due of less than)0. For additional information, get Publication 5, Tax Withholding and Estimated Tax.

A. Who Must File.—The rules below are for s, citizens or residents and citizens of Puerto Rico, Virgin Islands, Guam, or American moa. If you are a nonresident alien, use Form 40-ES(OIO). You must make a declaration if ur estimated tax is $100 or more AND:
(1) Your expected gross income for 1981 includes more than $500 in income not subject to hholding, or

(2) Your expected gross income is more than:
● $20,000 if you are single, a head of household, or qualifying widow or widower.
● $20,000 if you are married, can file a joint declaration, and your spouse has not received wages for 1981.
● $10,000 if you are married, can file a joint declaration, and both of you have received wages for 1981.
● $5,000 if you are married and cannot file a joint declaration.

Note: If you must file a declaration, you may be having enough tax withheld during the ar. To avoid making estimated tax payments xt year, consider asking your employer to take re tax out of your earnings. To do this, file ew Form W-4, Employee's Withholding Allowe Certificate, with your employer and make e you will not owe $100 or more in tax. You also may have tax withheld from certain anty or pension payments you receive. To do file Form W-4P with the payer of the annuity.

3. How to Figure Your Estimated Tax.—Use Estimated Tax Worksheet on page 2 and ur 1980 tax return as a guide for figuring your imated tax.

Most of the items on the worksheet are self-planatory. However, the instructions below wide additional information for filling out certn lines.

Line 7—**Additional taxes.**—Enter on line 7 y additional taxes from:
● Form 4970, Tax on Accumulation Distribution of Trusts,
● Form 4972, Special 10-Year Averaging Method,
● Form 5544, Multiple Recipient Special 10-Year Averaging Method,
● Form 5405, Recapture of Credit for Purchase or Construction of New Principal Residence, OR
● Section 72(m)(5) penalty tax.

Line 12—**Self-employment tax.**—If you and ur spouse file a joint declaration and both ve self-employment income, figure the estimated self-employment tax separately. Enter the al amount on line 12.

Line 15(a)—Earned income credit.—Generally, you may be allowed this credit if you are married and entitled to a dependency exemption for a child living with you, if you are a surviving spouse, or if you are a head of household. Earned income includes wages, salaries, earnings from self-employment, etc. Figure the credit as follows:

(1) 10% of earned income, but not more than $500		$500
(2) Limitation		
(3) Earned income or adjusted gross income, whichever is larger		
(4) Less	$6,000	
(5) Subtract line 4 from line 3 . . .		
(6) 12½% of line 5		
(7) Subtract line 6 from line 2 .		
(8) Earned income credit. Enter line 1 or line 7, whichever is smaller		

Note: You must reduce the amount above by any advance earned income credit payments received from your employer.

Caution: Generally, you are required to itemize your deductions if:
● you have unearned income of $1,000 or more and can be claimed as a dependent on your parent's return,
● you are married filing a separate return and your spouse itemizes deductions,
● you file Form 4563, OR
● you are a dual status alien.

For more information, see Schedule TC (Form 1040). If you must itemize and line 2b of the Estimated Tax Worksheet is more than line 2a, subtract 2a from 2b. Add this amount to line 1 of the worksheet and enter the total on line 3. Disregard the instructions for line 2c and line 3 on the worksheet.

C. How to Use the Declaration-Voucher.—
(1) Enter your name, address, and social security number in the space provided on the declaration-voucher.
(2) Enter the amount shown on line 17 of the worksheet in Block A of the declaration-voucher.
(3) Enter the amount shown on line 1 of the worksheet on line 1 of the declaration-voucher.
(4) If you paid too much tax on your 1980 Form 1040, you may have chosen to apply the overpayment to your estimated tax for 1981. If so, enter in Block B the overpayment from 1980.

You may apply all or part of the overpayment to any voucher. Enter on line 2 the amount you want to apply to the voucher you are using. Subtract line 2 from line 1 and enter the amount of the payment on line 3. If you are filing a declaration (or an amended declaration), mail it to the Internal Revenue Service even though line 3 is zero. File the remaining vouchers only when line 3 is more than zero.

(5) Sign the declaration-voucher and tear off at the perforation.
(6) Attach your check or money order to the declaration-voucher. Make check or money order payable to "Internal Revenue Service." Please write your social security number and "Form 1040-ES—1981" on your check or money order. Please fill in the Record of Estimated Tax Payments so you will have a record of your past payments.

For each later declaration-voucher, follow instruction (1) above, fill in lines 1, 2, and 3 of the form, attach check or money order, and mail.

D. When to File and Pay Your Estimated Tax.—The general rule is that you must file your declaration by April 15, 1981. You may either pay all of your estimated tax with the declaration or pay in four equal amounts that are due by April 15, 1981; June 15, 1981; September 15, 1981; and January 18, 1982. Exceptions to the general rule are listed below:

(1) **Other declaration dates**—In some cases, such as a change in income, you may have to file a declaration after April 15, 1981. The filing dates are as follows:
● **June 15, 1981,** for changes between April 1 and September 2.
● **September 15, 1981,** for changes between June 1 and September 2.
● **January 18, 1982,** for changes after September 1.

You may pay your estimated tax in equal amounts. If the first declaration-voucher you are required to file is:
Voucher No. 2, enter ⅓;
Voucher No. 3, enter ½;
Voucher No. 4, enter all;
of line 17 on line 18 of the worksheet and on line 1 of the declaration-voucher.

(2) **Your return as a declaration.**—If you file your 1981 Form 1040 by February 1, 1982, and pay the entire balance due, then you do not have to—
● file the required amended declaration due on January 18, 1982.
● file your first declaration which would be due by January 18, 1982.
● make your last payment of estimated tax.

(3) **Farmers and fishermen.**—If at least two-thirds of your gross income for 1980 or 1981 is from farming and fishing, you may do one of the following:
● File your declaration by January 18, 1982, and pay all your estimated tax.
● Or file Form 1040 for 1981 by March 1, 1982, and pay the total tax due. In this case, you do not need to file a declaration for 1981.

(4) **Fiscal year.**—If your return is on a fiscal year basis, your due dates are the 15th day of the 4th, 6th, and 9th months of your fiscal year and the 1st month of the following fiscal year. If any date falls on a Saturday, Sunday, or legal holiday, use the next regular workday.

(Continued on page 4)

Amended Declaration Schedule			Record of Estimated Tax Payments				
se if your estimated tax changes after you file your declaration.)			1040-ES number	Date	Amount	1980 overpayment credit applied	Total amount paid and credited (add (b) and (c))
Amended estimated tax. Enter here and in Block A on declaration-voucher				(a)	(b)	(c)	(d)
Less:							
(a) Amount of 1980 overpayment chosen for credit to 1981 estimated tax and applied to date . .			1				
(b) Estimated tax payments to date . . .			2				
(c) Total of lines 2(a) and (b) . . .			3				
Unpaid balance (subtract line 2(c) from line 1) . . .			4				
Amounts to be paid (line 3 divided by number of remaining filing dates). Enter here and on line 1 of declaration-voucher . .			Total . . . . ▶				

1981 Estimated Tax Worksheet (Keep for your records—Do Not Send to Internal Revenue Service)

1 Enter amount of Adjusted Gross Income you expect in 1981 . . . .

2 a If you plan to itemize deductions, enter the estimated total of your deductions. If you do not plan to itemize deductions, skip to line 2c and enter zero . . . .

            \$3,400 if married filing a joint return (or qualifying widow(er)) . . . . . .

  b Enter \$2,300 if single (or head of household) . . . .

            \$1,700 if married filing a separate return . . . .

  c Subtract line 2b from line 2a (if zero or less, enter zero) . . . .

3 Subtract line 2c from line 1 . . . .

4 Exemptions (multiply \$1,000 times number of personal exemptions) . . . .

5 Subtract line 4 from line 3 . . . .

6 Tax. (Figure tax on line 5 by using Tax Rate Schedule X, Y or Z in the 1980 Form 1040 instructions) . . . .

7 Enter any additional taxes from instruction B . . . .

8 Add lines 6 and 7 . . . .

9 Credits (credit for the elderly, credit for child care expenses, investment credit, residential energy credit, etc.) .

10 Subtract line 9 from line 8 . . . .

11 Tax from recomputing a prior year investment credit . . . .

12 Estimate of 1981 self-employment income \$.............................; if \$29,700 or more, enter \$2,762.10; if less, multiply the amount by .093 (see instruction B for additional information) . . . .

13 Tax on premature distributions from an IRA . . . .

14 Add lines 10 through 13 . . . .

15 (a) Earned income credit (see instruction B) . . . .

    (b) Estimated income tax withheld and to be withheld during 1981 . . . .

    (c) Credit for Federal tax on special fuels and oils (see Form 4136 or 4136–T) . . .

16 Total (add lines 15(a), (b), and (c)). . . . .

17 Estimated tax (subtract line 16 from line 14). If \$100 or more, fill out and file the declaration-voucher; if less, no declaration is required at this time . . . .

18 If the first declaration-voucher you are required to file is Number 1, due April 15, 1981, enter ¼ of line 17 here and on line 1 of your declaration-voucher(s) . . . .

  Note: *If you are not required to file Voucher No. 1 at this time, you may have to file by a later date. See instruction D(1).*

Page 2

SCHEDULE SE (Form 1040)	**Computation of Social Security Self-Employment Tax** ▶ See Instructions for Schedule SE (Form 1040). ▶ Attach to Form 1040.		**19 80** 23
Department of the Treasury Internal Revenue Service			

Name of self-employed person (as shown on social security card)		Social security number of self-employed person ▶			

Part I   Computation of Net Earnings from FARM Self-Employment

Regular Method

Net profit or (loss) from:			
a Schedule F (Form 1040)	1a		
b Farm partnerships	1b		
Net earnings from farm self-employment (add lines 1a and 1b)	2		

Farm Optional Method

If gross profits from farming are:

a Not more than $2,400, enter two-thirds of the gross profits . . . . }	3		
b More than $2,400 and the net farm profit is less than $1,600, enter $1,600			
Enter here and on line 12a, the amount on line 2, or line 3 if you elect the farm optional method .	4		

Part II   Computation of Net Earnings from NONFARM Self-Employment   **SE**

Regular Method

Net profit or (loss) from:			
a Schedule C (Form 1040)	5a		
b Partnerships, joint ventures, etc. (other than farming)	5b		
c Service as a minister, member of a religious order, or a Christian Science practitioner. (Include rental value of parsonage or rental allowance furnished.) If you filed Form 4361 and have not revoked that exemption, check here ▶ ☐ and enter zero on this line	5c		
d Service with a foreign government or international organization	5d		
e Other (specify) ▶..	5e		
Total (add lines 5a through 5e)	6		
Enter adjustments if any (attach statement, see page 29 of Instructions)	7		
Adjusted net earnings or (loss) from nonfarm self-employment (line 6, as adjusted by line 7) . .	8		

Note: If line 8 is $1,600 or more or if you do not elect to use the Nonfarm Optional Method, skip lines 9 through 11 and enter amount from line 8 on line 12b.

Nonfarm Optional Method

a Maximum amount reportable under both optional methods combined (farm and nonfarm) . .	9a	$1,600	00
b Enter amount from line 3. (If you did not elect to use the farm optional method, enter zero.) . .	9b		
c Balance (subtract line 9b from line 9a)	9c		
Enter two-thirds of gross nonfarm profits or $1,600, whichever is smaller	10		
Enter here and on line 12b, the amount on line 9c or line 10, whichever is smaller	11		

Part III   Computation of Social Security Self-Employment Tax

Net earnings or (loss):			
a From farming (from line 4)	12a		
b From nonfarm (from line 8, or line 11 if you elect to use the Nonfarm Optional Method) . . .	12b		
Total net earnings or (loss) from self-employment reported on lines 12a and 12b. (If line 13 is less than $400, you are not subject to self-employment tax. Do not fill in rest of schedule)	13		
The largest amount of combined wages and self-employment earnings subject to social security or railroad retirement taxes for 1980 is	14	$25,900	00
a Total "FICA" wages (from Forms W–2) and "RRTA" compensation	15a			
b Unreported tips subject to FICA tax from Form 4137, line 9 or to RRTA	15b			
c Add lines 15a and 15b	15c		
Balance (subtract line 15c from line 14)	16		
Self-employment income—line 13 or 16, whichever is smaller	17		
Self-employment tax. (If line 17 is $25,900, enter $2,097.90; if less, multiply the amount on line 17 by .081.) Enter here and on Form 1040, line 48	18		

☆ U.S. GOVERNMENT PRINTING OFFICE : 1980—O-313-070

1040 Department of the Treasury—Internal Revenue Service
U.S. Individual Income Tax Return **1980**

Privacy Act Notice, see Instructions | For the year January 1–December 31, 1980, or other tax year beginning _____ 1980, ending _____ 19___

Your first name and initial (if joint return, also give spouse's name and initial)	Last name	Your social security number

Present home address (Number and street, including apartment number, or rural route) | Spouse's social security no.

City, town or post office, State and ZIP code | Your occupation ▶ | Spouse's occupation ▶

Presidential Election Campaign Fund

Do you want $1 to go to this fund? . . . . | Yes | No | Note: Checking "Yes" will not increase your tax or reduce your refund.
If joint return, does your spouse want $1 to go to this fund? . . . | Yes | No

Requested by Census Bureau for Revenue Sharing ▶

A Where do you live (actual location of residence)? (See page 2 of Instructions.) State: City, village, borough, etc. | **B** Do you live within the legal limits of a city, village, etc.? ☐ Yes ☐ No | **C** In what county do you live? | **D** In what township do you live?

Filing Status
Check only one box.

1 ☐ Single
2 ☐ Married filing joint return (even if only one had income)
3 ☐ Married filing separate return. Enter spouse's social security no. above and full name here ▶ . . . .
4 ☐ Head of household. (See page 6 of Instructions.) If qualifying person is your unmarried child, enter child's name ▶
5 ☐ Qualifying widow(er) with dependent child (Year spouse died ▶ 19___). (See page 6 of Instructions.)

For IRS use only

Exemptions
Always check the box labeled Yourself. Check other boxes if they apply.

6a ☐ Yourself | ☐ 65 or over | ☐ Blind
b ☐ Spouse | ☐ 65 or over | ☐ Blind

Enter number of boxes checked on 6a and b ▶

c First names of your dependent children who lived with you ▶ ----------------------------------

Enter number of children listed on 6c ▶

d Other dependents: (1) Name	(2) Relationship	(3) Number of months lived in your home	(4) Did dependent have income of $1,000 or more?	(5) Did you provide more than one-half of dependent's support?

Enter number of other dependents ▶

7 Total number of exemptions claimed . . . .

Add numbers entered in boxes above ▶

Income
Please attach Copy B of your Forms W-2 here.

If you do not have a W-2, see page 5 of Instructions.

8	Wages, salaries, tips, etc.	8
9	Interest income (attach Schedule B if over $400)	9
10a	Dividends (attach Schedule B if over $400)_____, 10b Exclusion_____	
c	Subtract line 10b from line 10a	10c
11	Refunds of State and local income taxes (do not enter an amount unless you deducted those taxes in an earlier year—see page 9 of Instructions)	11
12	Alimony received	12
13	Business income or (loss) (attach Schedule C)	13
14	Capital gain or (loss) (attach Schedule D)	14
15	40% of capital gain distributions not reported on line 14 (See page 9 of Instructions) .	15
16	Supplemental gains or (losses) (attach Form 4797)	16
17	Fully taxable pensions and annuities not reported on line 18	17
18	Pensions, annuities, rents, royalties, partnerships, etc. (attach Schedule E)	18
19	Farm income or (loss) (attach Schedule F)	19
20a	Unemployment compensation (insurance). Total received _____	
b	Taxable amount, if any, from worksheet on page 10 of Instructions	20b
21	Other income (state nature and source—see page 10 of Instructions) ▶ _____	21
22	Total income. Add amounts in column for lines 8 through 21 . . . . ▶	22

Adjustments to Income
(See Instructions on page 10)

23	Moving expense (attach Form 3903 or 3903F)	23
24	Employee business expenses (attach Form 2106) . .	24
25	Payments to an IRA (enter code from page 10 ......) .	25
26	Payments to a Keogh (H.R. 10) retirement plan . . .	26
27	Interest penalty on early withdrawal of savings . . .	27
28	Alimony paid	28
29	Disability income exclusion (attach Form 2440) . . .	29
30	Total adjustments. Add lines 23 through 29 . . . . ▶	30

Adjusted Gross Income

31 Adjusted gross income. Subtract line 30 from line 22. If this line is less than $10,000, see "Earned Income Credit" (line 57) on pages 13 and 14 of Instructions. If you want IRS to figure your tax, see page 3 of Instructions . . . . ▶ | 31

GOVERNMENT PRINTING OFFICE 1980—O-313-237 95-0875140

Form **1040** (1980)

Form 1040 (1980)

Tax Computation (See Instructions on page 11)	**32** Amount from line 31 *(adjusted gross income)*	**32**	
	33 If you do not itemize deductions, enter zero . . . . } If you itemize, complete Schedule A (Form 1040) and enter the amount from Schedule A, line 41 . . .	**33**	
	Caution: If you have unearned income and can be claimed as a dependent on your parent's return, check here ▶ ☐ and see page 11 of the Instructions. Also see page 11 of the Instructions if: • You are married filing a separate return and your spouse itemizes deductions, OR • You file Form 4563, OR • You are a dual-status alien.		
	34 Subtract line 33 from line 32. Use the amount on line 34 to find your tax from the Tax Tables, or to figure your tax on Schedule TC, Part I . . . . Use Schedule TC, Part I, and the Tax Rate Schedules ONLY if: • Line 34 is more than $20,000 ($40,000 if you checked Filing Status Box 2 or 5), OR • You have more exemptions than are shown in the Tax Table for your filing status, OR • You use Schedule G or Form 4726 to figure your tax. Otherwise, you MUST use the Tax Tables to find your tax.	**34**	
	35 Tax. Enter tax here and check if from ☐ Tax Tables or ☐ Schedule TC	**35**	
	36 Additional taxes. (See page 12 of Instructions.) Enter here and check if from ☐ Form 4970, } ☐ Form 4972, ☐ Form 5544, ☐ Form 5405, or ☐ Section 72(m)(5) penalty tax . . .	**36**	
	37 Total. Add lines 35 and 36 . . . . ▶	**37**	
Credits (See Instructions on page 12)	**38** Credit for contributions to candidates for public office . . . **38**		
	39 Credit for the elderly (attach Schedules R&RP) **39**		
	40 Credit for child and dependent care expenses (*attach Form 2441*) . **40**		
	41 Investment credit (attach Form 3468) **41**		
	42 Foreign tax credit (attach Form 1116) **42**		
	43 Work incentive (WIN) credit (attach Form 4874) **43**		
	44 Jobs credit (attach Form 5884) **44**		
	45 Residential energy credits (attach Form 5695) **45**		
	46 Total credits. Add lines 38 through 45	**46**	
	47 Balance. Subtract line 46 from line 37 and enter difference (but not less than zero) . ▶	**47**	
Other Taxes (Including Advance EIC Payments)	**48** Self-employment tax (attach Schedule SE)	**48**	
	49a Minimum tax. Attach Form 4625 and check here ▶ ☐	**49a**	
	49b Alternative minimum tax. Attach Form 6251 and check here ▶ ☐	**49b**	
	50 Tax from recomputing prior-year investment credit (attach Form 4255)	**50**	
	51a Social security (FICA) tax on tip income not reported to employer (attach Form 4137) . .	**51a**	
	51b Uncollected employee FICA and RRTA tax on tips (from Form W-2)	**51b**	
	52 Tax on an IRA (attach Form 5329)	**52**	
	53 Advance earned income credit (EIC) payments received (from Form W-2)	**53**	
	54 Balance. Add lines 47 through 53 . . . . ▶	**54**	
Payments Attach Forms W-2, W-2G, and W-2P to front.	**55** Total Federal income tax withheld **55**		
	56 1980 estimated tax payments and amount applied from 1979 return . . **56**		
	57 Earned income credit. If line 32 is under $10,000, see pages 13 and 14 of Instructions **57**		
	58 Amount paid with Form 4868 . . . . **58**		
	59 Excess FICA and RRTA tax withheld (two or more employers) **59**		
	60 Credit for Federal tax on special fuels and oils (attach Form 4136 or 4136-T) **60**		
	61 Regulated Investment Company credit (attach Form 2439) **61**		
	62 Total. Add lines 55 through 61 . . . . ▶	**62**	
Refund or Balance Due	**63** If line 62 is larger than line 54, enter amount OVERPAID . . . . ▶	**63**	
	64 Amount of line 63 to be REFUNDED TO YOU . . . . ▶	**64**	
	65 Amount of line 63 to be applied to your 1981 estimated tax . . . ▶ **65**		
	66 If line 54 is larger than line 62, enter BALANCE DUE. Attach check or money order for full amount payable to "Internal Revenue Service." Write your social security number on check or money order . . ▶ (Check ▶ ☐ if Form 2210 (2210F) is attached. See page 15 of Instructions.) ▶ $	**66**	
Please Sign Here	Under penalties of perjury, I declare that I have examined this return, including accompanying schedules and statements, and to the best of my knowledge and belief, it is true, correct, and complete. Declaration of preparer (other than taxpayer) is based on all information which preparer has any knowledge. ▶ Your signature Date ▶ Spouse's signature (if filing jointly, BOTH must sign even if only one had income)		
Paid Preparer's Use Only	Preparer's signature and date ▶ Check if self-employed ▶ ☐ Preparer's social security no. Firm's name (or yours, if self-employed) and address ▶ E.I. No. ▶ ZIP code ▶		

SCHEDULE C Form 1040 Department of the Treasury Internal Revenue Service	**Profit or (Loss) From Business or Profession** (Sole Proprietorship) Partnerships, Joint Ventures, etc., Must File Form 1065. ▶ Attach to Form 1040 or Form 1041. ▶ See Instructions for Schedule C (Form 1040).	1980 09

Name of proprietor | Social security number of proprietor

Main business activity (see Instructions) ▶   ; product ▶

Business name ▶

Business address (number and street) ▶ ....   C Employer identification number
City, State and ZIP Code ▶

Accounting method: (1) ☐ Cash   (2) ☐ Accrual   (3) ☐ Other (specify) ▶ ....

Method(s) used to value closing inventory:

(1) ☐ Cost   (2) ☐ Lower of cost or market   (3) ☐ Other (if other, attach explanation) | **Yes** | **No**

Was there any major change in determining quantities, costs, or valuations between opening and closing inventory? . .

If "Yes," attach explanation.

Did you deduct expenses for an office in your home? . . . .

Did you elect to claim amortization (under section 191) or depreciation (under section 167(o)) for a rehabilitated

certified historic structure (see Instructions)? . . . .

(Amortizable basis (see Instructions) ▶   )

Part I Income

1 a Gross receipts or sales	1a		
b Returns and allowances	1b		
c Balance (subtract line 1b from line 1a)		1c	
2 Cost of goods sold and/or operations (Schedule C–1, line 8)		2	
3 Gross profit (subtract line 2 from line 1c)		3	
4 Other income (attach schedule)		4	
5 Total income (add lines 3 and 4) . . . . ▶		5	

Part II Deductions

6 Advertising		31 a Wages . .		
7 Amortization		b Jobs credit		
8 Bad debts from sales or services .		c WIN credit		
9 Bank charges		d Total credits		
10 Car and truck expenses		e Subtract line 31d from 31a .		
11 Commissions		32 Other expenses (specify):		
12 Depletion		a		
13 Depreciation (explain in Schedule C–2) .		b		
14 Dues and publications		c		
15 Employee benefit programs . .		d		
16 Freight (not included on Schedule C–1) .		e		
17 Insurance		f		
18 Interest on business indebtedness		g		
19 Laundry and cleaning		h		
20 Legal and professional services .		i		
21 Office supplies		j		
22 Pension and profit-sharing plans .		k		
23 Postage		l		
24 Rent on business property . . .		m		
25 Repairs		n		
26 Supplies (not included on Schedule C–1) .		o		
27 Taxes		p		
28 Telephone		q		
29 Travel and entertainment . . .		r		
30 Utilities		s		
33 Total deductions (add amounts in columns for lines 6 through 32s) . . . . ▶			33	

34 Net profit or (loss) (subtract line 33 from line 5). If a profit, enter on Form 1040, line 13, and
on Schedule SE, Part II, line 5a (or Form 1041, line 6). If a loss, go on to line 35 . . . . . | 34 |

35 If you have a loss, do you have amounts for which you are not "at risk" in this business (see Instructions)? . . ☐ Yes   ☐ No

SCHEDULE C–1.—Cost of Goods Sold and/or Operations (See Schedule C Instructions for Part I, line 2)

1 Inventory at beginning of year (if different from last year's closing inventory, attach explanation) .	1	
2 a Purchases	2a	
b Cost of items withdrawn for personal use	2b	
c Balance (subtract line 2b from line 2a)	2c	
3 Cost of labor (do not include salary paid to yourself)	3	
4 Materials and supplies	4	
5 Other costs (attach schedule)	5	
6 Add lines 1, 2c, and 3 through 5	6	
7 Inventory at end of year	7	
8 Cost of goods sold and/or operations (subtract line 7 from line 6). Enter here and on Part I, line 2 . ▶	8	

SCHEDULE C–2.—Depreciation (See Schedule C Instructions for line 13)
If you need more space, please use Form 4562.

Description of property (a)	Date acquired (b)	Cost or other basis (c)	Depreciation allowed or allowable in prior years (d)	Method of computing depreciation (e)	Life or rate (f)	Depreciation for this year (g)
1 Total additional first-year depreciation (do not include in items below) (see instructions for limitation)——▶						
2 Other depreciation:						
3 Totals				3		
4 Depreciation claimed in Schedule C–1				4		
5 Balance (subtract line 4 from line 3). Enter here and on Part II, line 13 . . . . ▶				5		

SCHEDULE C–3.—Expense Account Information (See Schedule C Instructions for Schedule C–3)

Enter information for yourself and your five highest paid employees. In determining the five highest paid employees, add expense account allowances to the salaries and wages. However, you don't have to provide the information for any employee for whom the combined amount is less than $25,000, or for yourself if your expense account allowance plus line 34, page 1, is less than $25,000.

Name (a)	Expense account (b)	Salaries and wages (c)
Owner		
1		
2		
3		
4		
5		

Did you claim a deduction for expenses connected with:	Yes	No
A Entertainment facility (boat, resort, ranch, etc.)?		
B Living accommodations (except employees on business)?		
C Conventions or meetings you or your employees attended outside the U.S. or its possessions? (see Instructions) . .		
D Employees' families at conventions or meetings?		
If "Yes," were any of these conventions or meetings outside the U.S. or its possessions?		
E Vacations for employees or their families not reported on Form W–2?